Sunshine and Rain at Once

Summer 81

To Ann + John Eberle
with fond memories of
our week together at
star Island!
                    Clarke Wells

ii

Sunshine and Rain at Once

by Clarke Wells

252.0836
WEL

Acknowledgements:

Two essays, "The Gross, Yes the Gross National Product" and "Identity, Identity, Who's Got the Identity" appeared in the *Unitarian-Universalist World* 2/15/71 and 5/15/71.

The selection "for A.C.S." is from *73 Voices* edited by Christopher Raible and Edward Darling, copyright 1972 by Unitarian Universalist Association.

Three poems, "His last mass chose an Irish sonnet," "Sine Nomine," and "Church towers and sky scrapers" first appeared in the Religious Arts Guild publication *Along with All the Other Onceloved Things*, edited by Jeanne Hill, copyright 1972 by the Worship Arts Clearing House of the Unitarian-Universalist Association.

Two essays, "Super Patriot" and "Tribalism" appeared in the *Unitarian-Universalist World*, May 1, 1974 and Oct. 15, 1974.

The essay on "Aging" appeared in the *Unitarian Universalist Christian*, Summer/Autumn 1973.

The essay "Twinkle, Twinkle?" is from *The Tides of Spring*, edited by Charles Grady, 1973. Unitarian Universalist Association.

The poem "for pablo neruda 1904-1973" from *Neruda/Chile*, edited by Walter Lowenfels, Beacon Press, Boston, 1975.

The poem "Coitus" published in 1973 *Pyramid*, Issue 13, Ottone M. Riccio, editor, Hellric Publications, Jamaica Plain, Mass.

The poem "October," revised, appeared in *United Methodist Today*, Oct. 1974, Wm. C. Henzlik, editor, Ministry Section.

The selection "The Liberal Church" is from pamphlet *"Views of the Church,"* Unitarian Universalist Association.

Five columns, "Magician," "Obedience," "Messy Evangelist," "Snow," and "Atheism" first appeared in *From the Minister's Desk*, edited by Nance Hinnenkamp, St. John's Unitarian Church, Cincinnati, 1965.

"Valentine Wishes" appeared in the *Unitarian Universalist World* on Feb. 1, 1978; "Metrification" appeared in Dec. 15, 1977 issue of the same publication.

"Festival in the Church for JLA" appeared in "Kairos," Number 5, Autumn 1976.

ISBN 0-933840-10-1

Artwork by Judith C. Campbell

iv

Contents

II. Both, Both, My Girl

III. Banquet Prayers, Other Essays, Poems

IV. Uncollected Pieces

Foreword

Clarke Wells' trenchant writing has won him a wide readership. Part of his appeal is obviously his literate, pungent use of words. But his essays do more than glitter, they testify to the heights, depths, and in-betweens of life.

He writes frankly and dares to speak openly of feelings we all have, but rarely express. He also stands full in the prophetic tradition and does not fear to charge apathy, humbug, and cruelty, though compassion and forgiveness are ever-present themes. His writing is strong, yet tender; earthy yet soaring; affirming, yet accepting of brokenness. Clarke has a way of summing up humanness as we find it. We feel indebted to him for stating it for us so well.

We hope this present edition will introduce the writings of Clarke Wells to a new and wider congregation. We particularly thank Renee Adelman, G. Peter Fleck, Earl K. Holt III, Diane M.W. Miller, Anthony Friess Perrino, Christopher Gist Raible, Paul M. Smith, and John B. Wolf for their helpful support. We delight that many others will join us in keeping this volume at our desks, by the bedside, or in the travel case. We believe we share a special gift with you.

- Peter Spilman Raible

Preface

Dear Reader, a word about the shape of this booklet and the prejudices of its author. I am a Unitarian Universalist minister (for 26 years now though I find that hard to comprehend, even on rainy days). I believe in God, the Church, women's liberation, handball, the Red Sox, civil liberties, fruit trees and the sun.

I am a Christian humanist influenced by Marx and Shakespeare and I see our tiny and beloved denomination as one of the brother-sister-hoods within the Church Universal. To me the Church Universal is an institutional dream of a world, our earth, under justice and law and clean air, full of forgiveness, oranges, reconciliation; full of dancing and praise for the chance to be alive.

The title of this booklet is from the master's magic play, *The Tempest*. During student days my teacher, Anabaptist scholar Robert Friedmann (perpetual light shines on him or no one), one of Hitler's gifts to America, spoke in conversation with me about the tempests of life and the significance of Christian faith: "Vells, it is all *Sturm and Drang* and we must everyone be Christs helping button up the neighbor's coat."

I think the liturgical tradition of Lent is a gift, a garment for the storm, survival apparel. Our individual dyings and becomings are given a voice, wisdom and companionship in a story and heritage larger than the isolation and pain of our unconnected selves. We don't have to be "religious" or "Christian" to enter into Lent, only human. Since we're all in the club I invite you to join me in traversing together this season of faith, self-examination and hope. We have St. Francis's word that "Brother Ash is pure."

- Clarke Wells

The
Strangeness
of
This
Business

ASHES AND EASTER

In a culture where the plastic smile is mandatory and cheap grace abounds, the sober subject of ashes comes almost as refreshment. At least we know we start without illusions. All our minor triumphal entries end, like Lear, a ruined piece of nature upon the rack of this tough world.

The ashes of Ash Wednesday are mixed in a common bowl of grief. They are made from palm fronds used in celebration the year before at a brief hour of triumph, Palm Sunday. In the Catholic tradition the ashes are made into a paste and daubed on the foreheads of the faithful, a grey sign of execution that must preface any Easter.

John Bunyan said that the woman of Canaan, who would not be daunted, though called dog by Christ (Mat. 15:22) and the man who went to borrow bread at midnight (Luke 11:5-8) were, ultimately, great encouragements to him. They hung in there thru the dark days.

For religious liberals ashes can symbolize, too, the dying of the seed that it may be born, the place of the phoenix, and, yes, the dissolution of integrity so that deeper integrities may emerge. The divine creativity leaves ashes in its wake so that new worlds may rise up and adore. In the strangeness of this business Ash Wednesday is the opening to Easter.

MARCH WIND

The Romans knew what they were doing when they named March after the God of War. The month is bellicose, full of wind, mud, storms. It tempts with things vernal, but like any teasing that goes on too long, it irritates rather than inspires. April may be the "cruelest month," but militant March is offense enough. Embattled, we wait for spring.

> The winds of March are wild and strong
> They howl and whistle all day long
> They pull the hats from tall men's heads
> And frighten children in their beds

This song, the first I remember learning in childhood, says more than it says. Caesar was not the only one to miss the premonitions under the turbulent skies of March. It was understood by us that the tall man in the song who had his hat blown off was Mr. Lincoln, and that in later spring on Good Friday he would have it blown off for good. Lent, we learned, was the tough road to Easter, for Jesus and us all, the smell of lilac, the cost of tears.

Gethsemane and Golgotha may not be the end but, damn it, they are part of the way. I don't like the Ides of March, but I do know, though, that March's fury and sound are finally subsumed in a wholeness that comprehends the season's partial witness. Mars himself, I read somewhere, played a role in mythology beyond that of slaughterer. Strangely, he was also assigned to protect the fields.

And then there are the kites. March is the season of kites. And kites in their soaring and flight are ancient symbols of a risen Christ. It is worthy to note they fly in the turbulence and tempests of March.

TRAVELING LIGHT

A friend of mine says he'd travel more, but that he finds travel narrowing. This twist on the legendary broadening aspects of travel is not without wisdom. All of us have experienced the uncreative frustrations that travel sometimes entails. The images of the harrassed tourist, bags in hand, cameras flopping, grabbing for tickets, retrieving passports, arguing with porters, wife, luggage, and attempting to prevent his children from urinating on the dock, these images are nearly archetypal.

A traveler can have so much luggage about him that he cannot see beyond it. The vehicles for visitation interfere with the visit, the means of conveyance take over the purpose of the trip, the accoutrements become encumbrance, the servants master. The new country we would visit is shut off from view and any growing, creative interchange we would have with it is impossible.

So wrapped up with created goods (our luggages) and exhausted by them, we cut ourselves off from new country, of experience and values to be. Weighed down with what we own, we cannot enjoy or be open to any new thing. This, if you want it, is a definition of sin and idolatry: being weighed down with so much luggage we lose the purpose of the trip.

David went against Goliath leanly prepared. He did not accept the proffered armor. It would have been his death. And the saints? One of the tests for being a saint is the countenance of joy. And you've never seen a saint with much luggage (including the weight of needless worry, anxiety, guilt, pre-occupation with self).

The saints travel light. That way they can look and see and relate and heal. That way they can hear the music, and dance.

THE MAGICIAN

Once upon a time there was a magician who didn't know he was one because nobody every told him he was, and besides he had been taught from early childhood that magicians were not be taken seriously—they were trick players, prestidigitating, pretending to make things happen that can't happen, presuming to have special powers which everybody knows they don't have.

The magician (who didn't know he was) lived simply, minded his own business, and didn't say much and was good to his family and worked at his job as hard as you would expect an ordinary man to work at an ordinary job. When one day he died it was an ordinary sort of death and everybody came to his funeral because Rev. Poke always gave great funeral talks. Rev. Poke began with ''swelling prologues to imperial themes'' and ended on the same note, swelling.

Some time after the funeral the magician's children discovered a diary which they did not know their father had kept, and they opened it and a jaguar jumped out, and yards and yards of rainbow silk, desperate, beautiful, unwinding.

FALL OPENING

Welcome back to your Church. I hope you use it well—for worship, education, service and fellowship. Here may you tap into the best resources of our religious heritage and a freeing liberal tradition; take part in mind-quickening thought, heart-opening concerns, soul-stretching liturgy. Here may you tie in with your history and with humanity's struggling and dearest hopes; enjoy the companionship of a larger family in a larger house than any can separately have; give your voice resonance by joining it to others in singing and prayer and purpose beyond the single self.

The Church is to the single self what the belly of a guitar is to the single string. The single string unconnected, isolated, alone, is twangy, weak, somewhat pitiful, but when tied to a good frame and resonating with others it becomes, in Browning's words, "not a fourth sound but a star."

I must not urge you to attend Church, although I'm tempted because I know the strength in numbers and the reinforcement people can give each other. Shared experiences have an intensity and duration—reverberations, overtones—not given to solitude.

As far as I know Whitehead's statement that religion is what a man does with his solitude is the only dumb thing he ever said. Most men's private diaries are extremely boring, and that includes Thoreau. (That's the old one-two punch and first double heresy of my liberal Church year.)

Seriously, we come alive in groups. We shrivel without their dialectic demands. But God help us if these groups have no higher accounting than bowling scores or basket weaving. Our lives are trivialized unless kept under what Milton called the Great Taskmaster's Eye, opened to the Infinite, engaged to serious reckoning, bound to ancient sources and to the Great Becoming.

Welcome back to your Church.

WHEN THE
WAR DRUMS SOUND

We must say no one more time to our leaders—Republican, Democrat, or otherwise—who love too much the exercise of their power of the sword, who thrill overmuch at the clash of battalions dying under their command.

We must say no one more time to leaders who exploit our highest sentiments of patriotism and compassion to gain their ends.

We must say no one more time to leaders who lavish billions abroad to bolster corrupt and contemptible regimes, while malnutrition, sickness and despair stalk millions of our own at home.

We must say no one more time to leaders who want to rip apart and divide our people further just as our wounds have begun to heal.

We must say no one more time to leaders who call for more sacrifice while our own VA hospitals remain under-staffed and under-equipped to care for the paralyzed and disfigured and maimed who give out each day their last full measure of devotion to a cause that has brought us only bitterness and tears and the judgment of God.

We must say no one more time to leaders who refuse to see the polycentric character of communism, who persist in contending that our vital interest is served by twisting one world into two monstrous camps of hysteria and hate.

We must say no one more time to leaders who put their final trust in war, that institution Channing called "the concentration of all human crime," those leaders who in the name of national honor worship at the altar of death, deceit and the dehumanization of life.

So that healing and renewal can have a change to mark our bicentennial, so that the sun may shine to re-lighten our land and lure us back to hope, we must say no one more time, with our letters, our voices, our votes, and our lives, fortunes and sacred honor, say it again. No, one more time.

ADVICE OF A KID

Several years ago and shortly after twilight our 3½-year-old tried to gain his parent's attention to a shining star.

The parents were busy with time and schedules, the irritabilities of the day and other worthy pre-occupations. "Yes, yes, we see the star—now I'm busy, don't bother me." On hearing this the young one launched through the porch door, fixed us with a fiery gaze and said, "You be glad at that star!"

I will not forget the incident or his perfect words. It was one of those rare moments when you get everything you need for the good of your soul—reprimand, disclosure and blessing. It was especially good for me, that surprising moment, because I am one who responds automatically and negatively to the usual exhortations to pause-and-be-more-appreciative-of-life-unquote. Fortunately, I was caught grandly off guard.

There is a notion, with some truth in it, that we cannot command joy, happiness, appreciation, fulfillment. We do not engineer the seasons of the soul or enjoin the quality of mood in another, and yet, I do believe there is right and wisdom in that imperative declaration—you be glad at that star!

If we cannot impel ourselves into a stellar gladness, we can at least clean the dust from the lens of our perception; if we cannot dictate our own fulfillment, we can at least steer in the right direction; if we cannot exact a guarantee for a more appreciative awareness of our world—for persons and stars and breathing and tastes and the incalculable gift of every day—we can at least prescribe some of the conditions through which an increased awareness is more likely to open up the skies, for us and for our children.

It is not always the great evils that obstruct and waylay our joy. It is our unnecessary and undignified surrender to the petty enemies: and I suggest it is our duty to scheme against them and make them subservient to human decree—time and schedules, our irritabilities of the day, and other worthy pre-occupations. Matters more subtle and humane should command our lives. You be glad at that star.

IT OR THEE?

I've always liked John Calvin, even though he was a mean fellow, especially to Unitarians and Universalists and anyone else who disagreed with him. But he wasn't any meaner than most of his contemporaries. And from what I've read about Michael Servetus, the great Unitarian martyr, he wasn't exactly the kind of fellow you'd like to have around the house on a regular basis. Erasmus, yes; Calvin or Servetus, no.

But if it hadn't been for Mr. Calvin we would be without the greatest nutshell question and answer ever penned. "What is the chief end of man? To glorify God and enjoy his presence forever." There it is, everything.

Many might agree and say that, yes, this is a very well put statement, but hardly suited to our linguistically analyzed habitat, the non-theological world of scientific us. *Tout au contraire* (Calvin wrote in, among other languages, French) I think his language most appropriate to this age. What other century has demanded such brevity or such enjoyment as our own?

If God is Being then what other task should there be but to glorify and sing praises to what makes life possible? And, ecologically speaking, what an advantage to anthropomorphic language (although I'm not sure there is an other kind available to us). At least such language implies an I-Thou relationship with one another and with our universe. I-It relationships, devoid of communication, intimacy, communion, are responsible for the ecological mess our globe is in. To enjoy His presence—at least it provides the opportunity for human response to our universe rather than mechanism to mechanism, robot to robot.

Sometimes we think we advance in language. But by dehumanizing the Otherness we dehumanize ourselves. So here's to Calvin and Servetus who knew how to handle the Queen's English.

DEATH AND DYING

CAUTION: A movie being circulated for viewing among Unitarian Universalists on Death & Dying is hazardous to religious health.

It's called "How Could I Not Be Among You?" The movie deals with a solemn and moving subject: the dying of a young man, who narrates and lives out his own response to the sentence announced by his doctors. Our sympathy is immediate and total and would remain so, until we realize we are being presented with a theological tract on how to live and die in authentic fashion.

The answer is a sub-Christian, narcissistic, upper-middle-class mindless orgy of phony life-affirmation. Frolic in the flowers, run around naked in the sun, lose your identity by getting mixed up in the landscape, digging how luscious it all is. Simply a latemodel resurgence of paganism which, while it claims to worship life, is in fact committed to death: the death of gratitude, of dignity, courage, the death of agape, ethics, penitence, forgiveness, reconciliation, the death of community and caring, the death of rationality, the denial of reality.

You'd think that our tradition, priding itself on a commitment to honesty and rationality, would not be suckered into buying such nonsense. But perhaps our strongest point is our weakest. Having trained the brain we have neglected the deeper reaches, leaving our emotional musculature flabby and unfit for reckoning with the powerful non-rational elements in our experience.

The explorer Scott, knowing the end was near, wrote in his last journal that he would die in his tracks like an Englishman. He did. His last prayers were for the welfare of his wife, country, family. The post-mortem on our movie we do not see, but we should know the pitiful man divorced his wife, howled in a cabin in the mountains, and died without hope.

If you want a model for death and dying try Scott, try King, Scorates. Maybe someday we'll even get Unitarian Universalists to check out Christ. I am not arguing for martyrdoms, only that we try to live—and die—for something beyond our own skins.

DECLINING
THE RECLINE

I note by the new yearbook we are keeping in step with the general decline of mainline institutional religion in America.

Does this mean religion in America is dying? Far from it. I read an article in a recent "Penthouse" about new groups: scientology, witchcraft, macrobiotics, human potentials, pop zen, astrology, jesus freaks, hare krishna and other recent forms of infidelity. (The phrase was used against Emerson's transcendentalism.)

I am struck by man's incurable religiosity. It is no accident that these new movements should gain their popularity at the same time as a decline of interest for main-line institutional religion sets in. Nature is not alone in abhorring a vacuum. So does homo religioso. Sweep one religion out of the house and, lo, seven new ones fly in through the window.

The choice for individuals and cultures is never between religion and non-religion. It is only between what kind of religion. For man's thirst for meaning will be satisfied, willy nilly; we've a heart full of service for any Lure that promises a life over the ordinary, a transcendence over routinization, an opening into the Infinite.

And any traditional religion that ignores or belittles man's need for a transcendent reference, for ultimacy and intimacy and community in relation to it, is inviting decline and the emergence of new ways, or old ways renewed, often irrational, narrow and idolatrous.

As ye sow, however, so shall ye reap. In our tradition's systematic praise of individualism over community, rationality over food for the subconscious, polite pluralism over commitment (freedom over dedication), we invite a host of religious surrogates, substitutes, replacements.

Boredom, said Channing, is the one unbearable pain, and men will do anything to overcome the sense of mean, trivialized, routinized existence. Either organized religion communicates a serious sense of mission about the purpose of human life, provides a community of inquiry and action toward it, and a relationship to the Ultimate Reality which stands over against it, or it reduces itself to a state of spiritual vegetability.

We needn't worry about the decline of religious interest. What we do need to worry about is the theological task of discerning what interest, what traditions should claim our attention; and then provide the means—communal, liturgical, institutional—for keeping in touch with them.

LETTER TO MY SONS

A letter to my sons:

What I want to say before any grey advice, is simply thank you. Thank you for coming to live in our house. You have added beyond measure to your mother and me. And since our life was already rich before you came, that is saying plenty. I wish to communicate to you a deep and abiding hello. I love you more deeply I think than our culture or my hang-ups have every permitted me to say. So I say it now, for you and the whole world to know, thank you for being, you precious, incredible, beautiful, crazy bums.

Now I advise. Remember you are free. Though I've tried to affirm all kinds of determinisms (they are real) to get myself off the hook for the occasional mess I've made of things, it won't wash. You are partly free at least, therefore partly responsible for the person you become. You are artists working on your own creation, you. Sculpt, paint, dance, write, think, sing greatly. Express yourself, yes, but deeply. Avoid the shallows, the trivialities, and the mendacity that will suck out your soul if you leave it unguarded long. A beautiful world yes, but it stinks with sin.

Two. You will undergo someday, unless you fake it or dehumanize yourself, pain deeper than you believe is possible to experience. You will bear unspeakable grief. I hope you endure and I commend to you during those periods long walks, cursing, planting tulip bulbs, Bach, and holding close all night to a lady who gives a damn.

Three. Spend your reading time with major leaguers. As a young man I spent too much time with Hesse, Cummings, Kierkegaard, Freud. You'll do better with Shakespeare, Homer, the Bible, expecially the prophets. If you want to learn about what makes you tick, stay away from psychology departments (as close as you can come in academic life to quackery and occultism and still get credit). Read history, sociology, theology, give yourself to the arts, and spend some time in self-examination and Church. Subjectivism is for sentimentalists. Your interior is a miracle, but no more than the sheer presence of Africa or Australia or the sacrament of underwater where we snorkeled at Lake Buel. Don't get bogged down in *your* feelings, *your* beliefs. Honor the otherness. For joy.

Four. In my book orthodoxy is a synonym for stupidity, fear and self-righteousness. But beware lest the liberalism in which you have been nurtured become a synonym for self-congratulation, vacuity and lack of passion.

Five. My mother had the good sense to ask my brother and me to carry my father's body to his grave. I hope you keep that tradition going. At the memorial service don't let anybody in the Church until they put their right hand on the Bible (KJV) and swear "I solemnly promise to join in all six hymns and to sing louder than I have ever sung before." By God that congregation is going to sing.

Six. Please, no heavy feelings of obligation toward your mother or me. You have been pure gift in our lives. For God's sake—I think you are both overly conscientious—don't ever try to win one for the Gipper. If you lose you'll feel embarrassed; if you win you'll get superstitious. Do, if you want, someday, maybe, if you're so inclined and have the time, go ahead, yes—plant a wild plum tree for the old man.

THE OTHERNESS

Religion, said Schleiermacher, is the feeling of absolute dependence. During a great storm a few years ago in which the city I was in was paralyzed in function and service, we came close to what Schleiermacher defined as religious experience.

"The waters became hard like stone and the face of the deep is frozen.... He scatters hoarfrost like ashes; who can stand against his cold?" James Martineau, the great 19th century British Unitarian theologian, asked God not to come in flashing storm or bursting frown of thunder, but in the still small voice "of wakening love and wonder," But who is Martineau to tell the Almighty what do do? God's way, proclaims the prophet Nahum, "is in the whirlwind and storm, and the clouds are the dust of his feet."

During a great storm some of the awe, majesty, fear, break through the calm prepackaged life we usually lead. People died in that storm. The still, small voice of Martineau was blasted by the Otherness of creation, the *totaliter aliter*, the *ganz andere*, of which the young Barth used to speak.

God does great things, says Job: "For to the snow he says, 'Fall on the earth'; whether for correction, or for his land, or for love, he causes it to happen."

I believe in snowplows and shelter but I think occasional tempests are necessary to get us back into right relation, religiously speaking. Recognizing the Otherness is the beginning of wisdom.

HARVEST IS ADAGIO

It was at the end of February 1966 that I bade a happy farewell to my parish in Cincinnati, and then edged off into years of pain; when the darkness, unshakable depression and inner calamity which is illness began its descent into my soul. Thanks to a lot of help from my friends, I lived. But it took several years before I felt myself again. It happened one summer in the Berkshires where twenty years before as a student I had been on the staff of a therapeutic community—physician, heal thyself!

We lived on a lake, snorkeled daily, played pool, snapped beans, picked cucumbers, saw Santana, George Russell, Webster Lewis, Miles Davis; met Gunther Shuller, heard new music, talked with composers, attended rehearsals and performances of the Ninth, Berlioz's *Requiem* (enough to wake the dead), Shostakovich No. 5; went to Jacob's Pillow for the first time in seventeen years, introduced our sons to Ted Shawn; ate Somali cuisine, were served by Alice herself in Stockbridge, about a half a mile from the railroad track; went to plays and musicals, serious and farcical, art galleries the same; studied Impressionism and twenty-five Renoirs at Williamstown, fell in love with Monet's *Tulip Fields at Sassenheim near Haarlem,* bought a Picasso lithograph, *La Ronde;* preached at Gould Farm, waded in streams, read a book on utopian communities, a novel by C.P. Snow, two books on Beethoven, and Adams on Tillich. There were other things, between sweating out the feat that feeling better was all temporary, a mirage, panicking when the darkness would briefly descend again. There were the Marx Brothers, Buster Keaton, shopping (without fear of crowds), exploring dirt roads, chamber music, steel drum bands, sleeping, being with people I love.

There was no particular moment of miracle. Harvest, I discover, is adagio. Healing takes time. Harvest is not that moment on Thanksgiving Day when the last thermal-hided squash is pulled from its frost-tangled bed. No. Harvest goes on all the time. It began months ago (like healing, before our knowing, without our seeing, without our caring).

In hay already cut, June radishes, leaf, scallion, pea, in maples long delivered of seed and April's sweet sugar—the harvest works on, adagio. I greet you this autumn, wishing good harvest to you and all of us. With fondest hopes for the ones who cannot wait, or waiting cannot believe, or believing cannot find, or knocking cannot enter, or praying feel only despair. Harvest is adagio. Healing takes time. I give you my word.

HOMECOMING

I saw the Northwestern-Minnesota Homecoming football game in Evanston, Illinois on a perfect fall Saturday, clear and beautiful. I had come to the game to air out my brain from a week of seminars on the University of Chicago campus about the "crises of the contemporary situation."

The stadium seemed full of light—banners, mums, happy faces, gorgeous fall clothes. The two Big Ten bands were dazzling in the sun. Decked in purples, whites, gold, they strutted and danced on to the green field with that arrogance of creatures convinced that God created the world specifically for their pleasure and to hell with God if he didn't. They whirled and marched and pounded drums and made music of the kind that opens your skill with joy. At half-time the Northwestern band led the alumni and all the old grads in singing "I Can't Stop Loving You." I looked around through my dark glasses and didn't see a face without a handful of tears.

Such is the power of public liturgies, old songs, traditions, alma maters, the autumn splendor that is close to pain, homecomings mixing with memories and desire.

In autumn more than other times we face our destinies clearly—personal, social, historical. The ambiguity of life is never more fully upon us—our freedom and unfreedom, our choosing yet having been chosen, the fated limits of age, health, sex, family, job, the phase-out of options, the last terminus. All amidst the overwhelming glory of life, and it hits again as the band plays, our defiant beauty, locked in to a destiny, a festival of saying No and Yes all at once, accepting the autumn, singing to the whole sad, damn, wonderful business, I can't stop loving you.

AGING

There's not much to say in favor of aging, damn it all. It's about the dirtiest trick God plays on us. I remember when Martha Graham, the dancer, stepped down. Asked for a comment on her retirement, she refused to say the right things.

Instead she said she was bitter, angry at what age was doing to her body, her life. As an ex-athlete, nostalgic over my own green days of lemon breath and supple explosions of musculature, I liked her frank words. They made me feel less guilty about my own resentment at growing old.

Though the man of faith in me would say "Into thy hands I commend my aging, O God," the Faustus in me cries out "O slowly, slowly, horses of the night!" I move back and forth, sometimes more than once in the same day, between Dylan Thomas's "rage, rage, against the dying of the light" and Walt Whitman's mystical approval of the way the cosmos has been put together—"come lovely and soothing death."

In spite of the way God has devised for us to spend the second half of our lives—in a state of slow decomposition—I do have to acknowledge that it's his cosmos, not mine. Maybe it's best to follow Porky's advice to Churchy LaFemme when he whines about life's brevity: "Aw shudup, you're lucky to be here in the first place."

And I must admit that aging is not inherently all that bad. An unjust and sick American socio-economic system must take at least equal blame with God for the insult, insecurity and terror that accompany our aging.

I only hope to be lucky, and to work to improve the system. In my ministry I've had the chance over the years to look at many kinds of aging. A few persons I've known have been in old age terribly beautiful, dignified, inspiring. In my prayers I aim for that, to be like one of them.

SNOW

There are many ways to despise the world and one of the ways is to despise the snow.

I've tried to be cordial about this matter in the past, but Monday night was the last thaw. A newscaster referred to that incredible evening as a "vicious storm." That did it. "Vicious" means depraved, wicked, immoral, degenerate, corrupt.

An objective reporter would keep his own value judgements to himself, stick to the facts, and relay the simple truth, which is: "This day a miracle, astounding, intricate, fabulous, graces our land."

But no. We are taught to regard a foot of snow as if it were an assault of a raging plague. I write to say that avoiding "fuel-line freeze-up" is not the chief end of humankind, and to say further that we should not ignore the wisdom of children who know a gift when they see one. If snow were a catastrophe, they would tell us.

What we need is about three more feet of snow. Being snowbound once in a while is of immense benefit to the human spirit. It binds us again to the elements of earth, provides seclusion for healing of the wounds to all our asphalt idiocies and alienations, compelling us to re-engage the fundamentals and understand anew how wonderful are: roofs, walls warm inside, houses, families, parcheesi, soup in bright-labelled cans, children, time for thought, recalling friends, naming them. Yes, we could use more snow.

So down with the snow haters, the winter whiners, the anti-icicle ilk; down with those thoughless of the deaths of innocent snowmen, who would halt the cut of skates, the sizzle-sound of skis, the cold fresh air, the view from night's window. Down with those who curse the sky without a glance at the glory they deny.

Our forbears had a tougher time with the elements than we, but they knew how to respond to winter. They did not shiver, sob, denounce or put on doom. They lighted fires in large hearths, they went outdoors, put bells on their sleighs and accompanied the dancing snow with the sound of joy.

Praise, praise the glory in the whirling snow, precious the crystals to mighty tons! So be it with us.

NOAH'S GIFT

I'm glad our week of rain is over, even though I know the waters are from the grace of God: "He shall come unto us as the rain, there shall be showers of blessing."

But rain is like every other good in this world: ambiguous, a blessing mixed. In the same Bible we read that "For forty days all the fountains of the great deep burst forth and the windows of heaven were opened," and we nearly got wiped out.

In Cherrapunji, India it rains 450 inches a year and at some unpronounceable place in Chile a droplet .05. I can appreciate the prayer, "Dear God try to get it together and avoid extremes please if you don't mind."

Only in Camelot does the morning fog disappear by 9 a.m. And even when God tries to be fair—Matthew says he sends his rain on the just and on the unjust —perfidious humanity fouls it up: a marvelous and bad verse goes,

> The rain it raineth all around
> On just and unjust people
> But mostly on the just because
> The unjust have the just's umbrellas.

Some rain is good, for lovers to walk in and Gene Kelly to sing and dance in, but a week dampens the soul, depresses the spirit. Hemingway understood it. You remember Lt. Henry after the dirty trick on Cat Barkley and him—"he went out of the room and left the hospital and walked back to the hotel in the rain."

But now the sun is out again, and another New England fall is on the way. We couldn't have it without the rain. Also, I must remind myself, if it weren't for the rain there would be no rainbows, and if there were no rainbows Shakespeare couldn't have blown open the language by calling one of them "a rich scarf to our proud earth." We can take a week of rain for an explosion like that.

I AM A CHAMELEON

True religion, I believe with L. P. Jacks, is primarily an affair of gratitude. In a Pogo episode Churchy LaFemme sits wailing in the back of the rowboat after seeing a newspaper headline: Sun Will Burn Out in Three Billion Years Killing All Life! Churchy cries, "Woe is me, I am too young to die." Porky reprimands him. He says, "Shut up, you're lucky to be here in the first place." Porky is right. I hope my final word is praise.

On the other hand I feel fully what Santayana called this "great disaster of our birth." I have cursed God for his sadism. He didn't need to make us open to that much pain. Beyond that I think it is a very dirty trick to hold out such beauty and promise to creatures and then take it all away. I used to solve this problem by positing a finite God. But I no longer think God is finite. That Otherness is as about as omnipotent as you can get. I despise It for carrying to the dark shore so quickly so much that I love. But I believe in the forgiveness of sins and I may even let God out on parole some day. Maybe we can forgive each other, if the weather stays good. So while I am grateful for life, I also think it is an outrage. I don't like crosses.

I do like a dancing clown I bought for my young son Jared at Christmas some years ago. The clown, dressed in red vest, checkered trousers and flower in lapel, when wound up with the key, moves along and clangs the cymbals held in each hand. My boy, big on Jesus's birthday and the clown, shouted happily to him, "Dance for Jesus, buddy! Dance for Jesus!"

We keep the clown, a family tradition now, and on a Christmas eve bring him out. With Bach's *Oratoria* in the background, the clown, cymbals banging, parades against the night. And then the chameleon is cornered, there's no more colors to turn. I believe in that scene. Exeunt all eclecticism, and the disaster of our birth. Dance for Jesus, buddy, dance for Jesus.

EARTH DAY

Earth Day, Earth Day, what do you say, Earth Day? About time, the nick of time, before our recycled mismanagement clobbers us all. The saints touched the earth and named it God's habitation before ecology was a gleam in the post industrial eye; saints don't need cram courses on respecting the universe.

Even the flowers not yet up in April cold are full of Biblical praise: Solomon's seal, Bishop's caps, Jack-in-the-pulpits, and certain theologians in Dutchmen's breeches. Earth Day, for earth's sake; you bet Earth Day, or no day worth the having.

But don't kid yourself: this land does not belong to you and me; the gulf-stream waters are owned off shore by humble companies who couldn't care less about you or me or God or fish or ducks or beaches or Alaskan reaches; and the red wood forests are decorative timbers for California rapists in Brooks Brothers suits. Don't kid yourself. The saints are scarce.

We who are guests—all of us (ask Buddha, Lao Tse, Abul Kassim, Christ) who know the miracle of this place and talk of earth days, mustard seeds, lilies of the field, must claim the earth back again for God and the psalmists. What is required is to take power from the plunderers at GM who are good to their wives, Humble Chevron and their Senators for hire; to proclaim anew that God so loved the world, yes, buddy, the world!

Here on this earth, said handsome Jack on that cold and only inaugural, God's work must be truly our own. We must care about Earth because it signals hope here in this spring of our own late lives: the best bargain going—life for free in exchange for keeping uncluttered Thee.

O Father and Mother God, creator of heaven and earth, of thine only have we received. I pledge allegiance to the earth and the biosphere hereafter; and to the ecosystem on which it stands, one planet, indivisible, with water and air for all.

You bet Earth Day; all days worth the having; all days worth the living; all days worth the giving. Here in this miracle place.

THE MESSY EVANGELIST

Dear Sir:

I thought I could forget about you and the incident at the spring on August 15. I wrote you a letter then, but decided not to mail it because I was angry at the time. I put it in the wastebasket and thought that just blowing off steam on the typewriter was sufficient therapy. But seven months have passed and I'm still mad at you. So I'm writing you again.

Copies of your tract, "Are You Concerned About Heaven?"—some several hundred—were scattered all over the spring site near the farm we stayed at this summer. Copies were floating in the spring, on the road, grass, parking area, all over the place.

It so happens we like that spring. A month before my boys and I cleaned up all the junk around it—pop bottles, beer cans, broken glass, old shoes, candy wrappers, moldy sandwiches, bottle tops, tinfoil, wax paper, string, and many other items. We carried away four bushels of junk so we could enjoy the spring twice a day, on our walks back and forth from the farm to the swimming pool about a mile away.

I have read your tract and I think for all your big talk you are just what my five-year-old said you were: an uncoordinated litterbug. On top of that I add that you are a lousy theologian. You talk about the necessity of a certain kind of baptism and then proceed to make a slop jar out of a beautiful and mysterious spring. You quote a lot of Scripture about believing *on the name,* but you don't care about *the reality.* If you did you wouldn't have made such a mess. If you believed in the reality of His name, you would help children get a drink when they came by, or something like that, instead of spreading your mimeographed gobbledegook of world-hating well-poisoning.

The Scripture says God so loved the *world* (not just a bit of it, but the whole world) and by golly sir that includes the grass and wildflowers and water at our spring on the Maineville Road, U.S.A. I hope you get better. And, in my unloving attitude toward you, me too.

Yours truly,

A disgruntled cleric and spring lover

LIME TREE

I grew up with trees. Climbed in them, built huts in them, carved initials in them, hid behind them for hide-and-seek, enjoyed them. But I never really saw a tree until I was grown up. It was in Florida in the summer of 1961, in a back yard, that I saw my first tree: a lime tree, full of limes. I didn't believe it. I took a chair out to the lawn, sat down in front of it and watched that tree for two hours. Occasionally I'd talk to it, argue with it.

Listen, I said, I've just finished spending eight years of my life in philosophy and theology to get this business figured out, and now you come along. The lime tree just stood there, full of silence, juice. Finally I said to it the only thing that was left to say: Lime tree, you're something else.

Trees for me, along with the sun and the loveliness of women, symbolize just about everything in creation that is fabulous. In some ways trees are the best symbol, closer to us than the sun but not as mortal as ladies.

Sequoias are higher than football fields and a bristlecone pine in the Inyo National Forest is 4,600 years old. These oldest and largest of living things point to the infinite. In their beauty, mystery, stunningness, in their life-giving, nurturing, profligate generosity they can be compared only with the most fabulous things, like God, full of grace.

Trees. What would we have done without them? Fuel, houses, tables, tools, masts, paper. And that's only the beginning, and we hope, the ending of some uses. Think of chocolate. It's from a tree. And coffee, maple sugar. Coconuts, olive oil, corks, dyes, rubber, turpentine, quinine, camphor; and all the fruits you can carry in your arms, not one the same color or shape as the next; and walnuts, almonds, pecans; and allspice, cinnamon, cloves, nutmeg—All the trees of the fields, it says in the Bible, clap their hands and sing out at the presence of the Lord!

Trees preserve the land and plant life and animal life (deforested regions are subject to flood, erosion, desolation.) Leaf mold and roots soak up water, forests are reservoirs essential to our life. Trees breathe tons of water vapor back into the air, purified of carbon dioxide, the most incredible air-conditioner in the world. Trees cut glare, bring shade and coolness and the song of birds. An ordinary apple tree sends back 94 gallons of water a day, saves the soil, provides fresh air and showers us with fruit besides. I know few human beings who contribute this much to creation in a lifetime, let alone a season.

For these reasons the sound of saws is a malicious sound and no longer a harbinger of progress in these late years of our planet's need. We *should* get sick when we see a tree cut down to make room for another asphalt lot. For we witness an execution, a lynching by banal men, of what is precious and holy on this earth.

If we can't produce, contribute and give back to life as much as a tree in our lifetime, the least we can do is tie the hands of the executioner with the buzz saw in his grip. In the grand schemes and reciprocities of life even we mortals can be of some use.

AND GOD
GAVE MAN DOMINION

The renewal of the fur trade and trapping is enough to sicken the heart. Traps which guarantee days suffering and which are outlawed in England and other countries are here in common use. Beavers are drowned in them, other animals die more slowly, grawing off their own legs to free themselves from the steel barbs tearing at their flesh. Sometimes a week goes by before the trapper returns to kill his prey. The look of lonely horror on the face of one fox dying in a trap conjures up for me such pity I can not look at it long. The pity is partly for humankind, the sad, cruel, stupid lot of us for permitting this blasphemy against life to go on. Is this what we were given dominion for, to torture creatures who mean us no harm and whose deaths are not now needed for our sustenance and welfare?

I am no sentimentalist about animals. I like steak and I like it blood rare. What I don't like and what none of us should tolerate is the torture of any creature. We dehumanize ourselves and make a moral wasteland out of the garden given to our charge.

The trappers have to eat, don't they? Of course, and if starvation is the only option then their work is without blame. But that is not the only option for the richest society on the planet. If we can subsidize farmers for not growing cotton for Christ's sake we can subsidize trappers for not torturing animals.

Two things I can do, besides praying for the creatures in the night woods, and I hope you will join: write to your hired hands, state and federal, to protest and to get information on what can be done and what groups you can join to help. (Nothing good gets done without groups, not Shakespeare, not the Bible, not anything. The torture will stop as individuals move *institutionally* to stop it, and not before.)

Secondly, let's be particular about the furs we wear. And give it at least as much thought as we do the purchase of a wool suit or cotton dress. From here on out only sociopaths will sport on their backs the remnant horror of such loveliness and pain.

FLIP OVER GRAVEYARDS

At one time I thought Methodists were wrong in their stand against smoking —cheap moralism I called it, between graceful puffs of ardent anti-legalism. Of course it turned out the Methodists were right and I was wrong. I had to eat my words, which was only slightly less difficult than choking on my smoke.

Convictions, prejudices, we carry for half a lifetime are not easily given up. At least not by me. Recently I've had to give up another one. I used to think that cemeteries had to go—prideful luxury and waste of space I called them. Today I eat those words.

Cemeteries in greater Boston make up 35 per cent of the open space remaining in the area, and how that space is used! Two men studied this space last year and encountered 95 species of birds, including beyond robins, blue jays and starlings, the yellow-shafted flickers, ring-necked pheasants, mockingbirds, bobwhites, black-billed cuckoos, belted kingfishers, Wilson's warblers, rufous-sided towhees, and great blue herons.

It finally has dawned on me that these creatures have as much right to the sky as the high rises. And who is humankind to crowd out other inhabitants of "land-consuming" graveyards? Our investigators found in our greater Boston burial grounds the homes of raccoons, striped skunks, red foxes, woodchucks, flying squirrels, red squirrels, opossums, muskrats, cottontails. Not to mention garter snakes, turtles, newts, salamanders, toads, bullfrogs a variety of fish and other proliferations of God's creativity.

It turns out that what was once necropolis becomes the guarantor of life, a center of vitalism, an oasis of ecological sanity. The receptacle of death becomes the fountain of being—a home for birds and beasts and trees, and, according to our investigators, a place of jogging, Frisbee, hide-and-seek, hopscotch, card playing, berry picking, model plane flying, lunch eating, dog walking, relaxing and sleeping, and coming to terms with family and history by graveside visitation. Also, Marvell notwithstanding, the grave's a fine and pleasant place and many there do embrace.

It's not easy to change your mind—but let's hear it: Viva graveyards! Viva the larger wisdom that confounds our own!

SUPER PATRIOT

I'm what you'd call a super patriot. Any quarrels I've had with America are lovers' quarrels. My *amor patriae* is so great that it has led me to convictions that no nice liberal minister should have. For example, I can't stand hearing people rave about the Alps. It means they haven't been to Colorado. and I don't like rich Americans who live overseas, people who make their money here and then take off for Spain or Rome to avoid taxes, and check in every few years just to retain citizenship. I'd slap them with a fine for tax evasion and ingratitude. If they persist in their bigamous adulteries I'd take away their citizenship and deny them visitation rights. If people don't love their country enough to live in it, let them get the hell out.

And what a country. I love it, physically. I've swum in its waters from the coast of Maine to the tip of Florida and up the Olympic wilderness coast of the state of Washington. I've caught 40-lb. red snappers in the Gulf of Mexico and salmon off the mouth of the Columbia. I've canoed on the Potomac, slept in sulphur baths at Big Sur, forded the Mississippi at Lake Itaska, made sand castles on the shores of Lake Michigan. I've skin-dived for lobster in Key Largo and waded streams in the Berkshires. I've been in 49 states and preached in 25 of them. I've been to Valley Forge, Antietam, Vicksburg, cherished my pilgrimages to Monticello, Springfield and the Hermitage. Hell, I've even visited Harding's tomb in Marion, Ohio.

Of course super patriotism can go wrong. Samuel Johnson rightly called patriotism the last refuge of scoundrels. A crook can wrap himself in the flag, commit any crime, proclaim "I did it for my country" and end up convincing himself that he is a national hero and candidate for sainthood. Watch out for us flagwavers.

And I know the love of God must transcend the love of country. If it doesn't patriotism degenerates into idolatry and tribalism, the mad worship of what is finite and partial. The prophets are right.

This said however, I still confess the unguarded testimony of my love for this land and for the dream of dignity and freedom enshrined in its title deeds for humankind. Sweet land of liberty, of thee I sing. And the more trouble you get in and the worse off you get the more I'm going to love you, even fight for you. Though I despise your wickedness, your racism, your corruption, your economic injustices, you're mine. You're the only one. You're beautiful. Super patriot, that's me.

TWINKLE, TWINKLE

I have decided against the stars. That's right, the stars, the twinkle-twinkle ones in the sky, like unto diamonds. This song from childhood is our basic indoctrination, our national anthem to the Infinite. We are taught it when we are little to keep us from getting nervous when we go outdoors.

"Twinkle, twinkle, little star"—*little* star! O the lightyear lies we tell to get rid of the shakes, fabricating from out of the darkest canopy a grandmotherly quilt to cover us. You'd think that sighting a star would be a foolproof antidote to our puffing pride. Our businesses and loves, the number of barns we own, the esteem in which we're held, our conceits of accomplishment—these should disappear after the briefest glance at the Pleiades.

But inventive, comic man prefers to strut against a backdrop more manageable. He constructs a Cassiopeian chair, and a dipper no larger than a human hand can hold to drink from. He sees not a night without roof, but twin brothers with winsome Latin names. He sees galaxies as domestic and nutritious as a Milky Way.

Well, I don't believe it. In a fit of theological honesty last night, the last twinkle twinkled away, and I am ready to say: I find the stars chilly, puzzling, and irrelevant to the central tasks of humankind.

I enjoy the rectangular lights from windows of human homes more than any whirling circles from planetary heights; I choose a single candle over all the splendor in the night sky; a burning hearth over all the stars God ever made. Flint is more holy than moonstone, matches more hallowed than meteors, the soft-glo bulb in my living room more precious than Arcturus. I prefer real roofs, though frail: the ones over my house, tent, church. Sleeping under the stars is for the blue-birds, or the brave.

REJOICE/LAETARE

Unrelieved gloom is foreign to the spirit of Judaism and Christianity. The world-despising sobriety of some sects is anti-biblical as well as anti-life.

Joy will not be gone, even from the darkest weeks of Lent. The name Lent itself is an early word for Spring, and this particular Sunday in Lent, mid-point in the calendar from Ash Wednesday to Easter, demonstrates that the joy of faith will not be put down. "Laetare" is the opening word of the Introit, "Rejoice, O Jerusalem." In the ancient Church on this Sunday in Lent flowers again appeared on the altar, organ music was played again. Laetare Sunday, an oasis in the wilderness, joy breaking through amidst the most solemn of journeys.

People in difficulty, namely most of us, need to know that it is all right to be joyful in spite of the pain that besets the human. way.

Laetare, the Fourth Sunday in Lent, is, in my book, one of the best Sundays in the year.

GIBRAN CAN
JUMP IN THE LAKE

Grief, said the poet, is a grievous thing. And Lent is the reminder in Christian faith of authentic life as pain. Writes Swinburne, we are transitory and hazardous, slight things and light. A little fruit a little while is ours, and the worm finds it soon.

Jesus, we are told, went the true way: to a cross. We have secular variations on a similar theme. Gibran (though love crucify you, follow him), encounter groups (let it all hang out, though you're as vulnerable as a clam to the abrasions of hurled sand), and all romantic philosophy that praises the virtue of risk (the hazarding of oneself in openness again and again, in spite of the accompanying hurt).

All this is true, but there is another side. You might say a paradox, a polarity, a dialectic truth opposite. And that is we should not open ourselves constantly to risk and pain and engagement. Flowers need to reach for the sun. They also need to protect their roots. If they don't they die and all that surrounds them is consumed.

The good life requires the pursuit of opposite values: freedom yes but also order; independence but also responsibility; going out to others, also care of oneself; engaging the world and retreating from the world; risking and refusing to risk; and all the rhythms of opposites in our lives—sleep and rising, work and play, intense concentration and careless rapture, considered planning and spontaneous insight, opening doors and closing them, the demands of justice and the claims of forgiveness; all ancient rhythms of yin and yang, life and death, giving and receiving, night and day, light and shadow.

I do not dispute the truth of the Lenten myth, but I want to affirm people who feel ashamed of their need *not* to risk, *not* to open to hurt, *not* to be reckless of pain or scornful of consequence. Kahlil Gibran can get crucified all he wants but I am for mortals who have been stung enough, who respect their thresholds of suffering.

Church history records minor sects who believed Jesus escaped the cross. This variant myth persists in Lawrence, and in a tiny group in Japan who think Jesus made it across to their island and lived as long as Socrates and died in good old age.

These stories aren't true. But they are all right. If Jesus, as I sometimes fancy, ducked out of Jerusalem after supper that Thursday night, got a girl, took off to another town, settled down and played parcheesi and went to the movies every Saturday for the rest of his life, that would be O.K. with me.

And I bless any of you who can't take too much, who decide there are enough crucifixions without looking for them, who need to go to the movies.

In life's dialectic the risk of pain is required. but so is pulling back in self-protection. Let us honor both requirements. And once in a while look at the truths in the heresy of minor myths, and even tell old Gibran to occasionally go jump in the lake.

WHAT IS A SACRAMENT?

What is a sacrament? A sacrament is anything you believe to be holy. Whatever for you is set apart, solemn, breathtakingly special—that is a sacrament.

Sacraments are old and new. They occur inside churches and out. Weddings and their joys are not confined to place, nor is a funeral and its grief. We christen (name, welcome, dedicate) a baby in ceremony, but in less formal ways, too—in our laughter, in touching our palms over a quickening life within, in our prayers, in kissing the newborn. These moments also are consecrating, dedicatory, celebrative. Sacramental.

A sacrament can be traversing the bridge at Golden Gate, walking at Gettysburg, viewing earth from the Canadian Rockies, strolling near crashing waves on sunlit coasts, or in the silence of sequoias; wading the brook in Minnesota where the Father of Waters begins its journey to the Gulf. A sacrament is reading the Second Inaugural at the Lincoln Memorial or listening there to Martin Luther King, or working a garden, or praying in our Gethsemanes.

Sacraments hover around the essentials of life, in such things as sexual intercourse and other deep reunions of flesh and spirit, in meals together, a last supper, at an altar rail with bread and wine or a picnic with strawberries and milk. Sacraments occur when the depth of life is disclosed.

Sometimes all life becomes sacramental. We walk on holy ground, the divine is present, interfused. We celebrate it, call it Thou.

These moments of sacred recognition flee and the world retreats to dreariness, as do we. But men and women and artists remember—to give liturgical shape, ceremonial form, some permanent hallowing to the sacredness we do meet in life. We recall, reclaim and transmit our times of sacred memory, the holy events and places of our lives, history and traditions.

Sacraments are very special because through them we enter the mystery and holiness of our common life, and see a vision of God.

DIALECTIC

People who believe in God are infantile.
People who don't believe in God are narcissists.

QUIZ TO TELL IF YOU'RE DEAD

A quiz on How to tell if you're dead: (check by each number if you agree with the sentiment expressed.)

1 I don't like the city
2 I don't care what happens as long as I'm left alone
3 I don't get angry
4 I don't get excited by beautiful women/men
5 I don't like conflict
6 I don't judge other people, no matter what
7 I don't feel guilty
8 I don't feed birds
9 I don't like children
10 I don't feel overwhelmed by anything
11 I don't like the country
12 I don't sing

If you checked all 12, or more than 7, Congratulations! You're dead! And without all the added fuss and expense of going to a mortuary.

If you checked between 3 and 7, Congratulations anyway! You're comatose, on the way!

If you checked 2 or less, sorry. I offer condolences. You're alive, with all the inconvenience that entails. To improve your score you might try hanging around doornails or sleeping in a refrigerator.

I BLOW A
SCOTTISH SHOFAR

I blow a Scottish shofar and resolve for every new year:
  To remember that new beginnings are actually possible.
  To stop beating myself for not living up to my potential.
  To be kinder, especially to the people I love most, my wife and
      two sons.
  To jog regularly.
  To stop worrying about the future so much.
  To start saving money for a piece of land and a house someday.
  To drink more fresh orange juice, less booze.
  To stop fantasizing about what I'd do if I won the million-
      dollar sweepstakes.
  To fantasize more about how to save the Church and western
      civilization.
  To work against the Nixons of this world, all that they stand
      for.
  To not allow my weariness and sophistication to overcome my
      indignation at the wickedness around me. America
      is at a midnight in morality.
  To lose weight and study French poets.
  To keep a wary eye on my limitations, to outgrow rather than
      indulge them.
  To while I'm shaving in the morning throw a kiss into the
      mirror once in a while, what-the-hell, why not.
  To not allow bourgeois conformists to make me timid or nutty
      avant-gardists to make me irresponsible.
  To do more of the things I love: studying, writing, dancing,
      singing, athletics; and less of the things I like least:
      worrying, stewing, envying, whining, reminiscing.
  To not go into my shell when my ideas get gunned down or my
      feelings get hurt.
  To stay as open and radical and fanciful as I can and pay the
      price.
  To not get mesmerized until midnight in front of some lousy
      TV show.
  To cease grieving that my garden—with the exception of a few scrawny
      tomatoes—was a complete failure, no squash, no cucumbers, no
      peas, no onions, no herbs; and to work on my great compost pile
      and think about next spring.
  To remember that most people are as neurotic, unfulfilled,
      incompetent, lazy and scared as I am.
  To yell thank you for the gift of the sun.

LAST ROUND-UP
FOR WM BOYD

hopalong cassidy
cashed in today
not sasparilla
not topper
could delay his away

with maynard and mix
he's quite defunct
spurs and chaps
to those far west bunks

these ten gallon riders
with silver screen clout
were meant to inspire
so when they check out
—ouch
we expire

SUNDAY MORNING

Sunday morning at the Goya show
  an aviator transmogrifies into a bat
  a ghoul woman tears teeth out of a hanged man's mouth
  a blinded prisoner slumps over his ropes, post
  a naked man, a surprised sheath, stares impaled
      on a battled tree
  on his stool a priest sits tightly, garroted
  a guard vomits over a pile of the dead
  Goya captions "This Is What You Are Made For"

We drive home, roof down, to our yard
  plant crocus bulbs, tulip
  walk in the woods in the clear creek bed
  turn on the Bears and Saints, call in neighbors
     for drinks
  charcoal broil in the autumn sun,
  send for whipped-cream pastries, plum tarts
  sprawl on the rug with mugs of coffee and
     the friendly *Times*
  reach at low rate the children at Cornell
  and in the crystal night hasten to make love
  as casually as we can

SOLERA

the madeira
we drank
festive by fire

40%
purpled in vats
off portugal
before the dead lived
150 yrs ago

we've an age
in our gut
my dear
a billion graves
several empires
convene at our throat
use our canals
and circuit our brief vineyards
sauntering
sloshing
drowning us

MEDICI TOMB

in the blown heat and damp
these faces will not say,
over forty, posed, snow-scuffed,
a few defiantly dyed,
in the twilight of the 6:15 bus
this midwinter morning to work
they will not say

beyond the usual peelings from beds,
yellow, sweet or stale,
beyond the necessities of toilets, prayer,
scales, pushing toaster levers down,
coughing, cylinders of frozen orange,
they will not say

they were handpicked by Lorenzo and Giuliano
or the master himself

Auroras, Crepuscolos, Giornos, Nottes,
in the half light
traversing into morning

BERMUDA

mini-England
tucked in the permanent and measured sun
lifts up coral, oleander,
birds of paradise,
calico loquats,
grapefruit, implosions of sun
in their advantages of high green

morning glories slope down
to the trimmed sand and Spanish bayonet,
the waters transfigure softly in the sieving reefs,
fountains of turquoise, aqua,
beaching where the suntanned loll

here in 1683
Sarah Bassett, slave,
for witchery and
poisoning her English lords
was burned alive at night

her cries sprang out red
and Bermuda was wide as terror

SECRETS

Between Wake and Midway and Hawaii
in 1968
a Russian sub
with a crew of 80
foundered at 17,000 ft

seven years later our CIA
with a 320 ft. craft
used grappling irons
and camouflaged cranes
to pull the sub up

the sub rose half way
until it broke in two
spilling classified
communist machinery
back to the bottom

expelling upward
only the cooled bodies
of eighty waving Russians
their teeth grinning
and wallets still in their pockets

FOR PABLO NERUDA
1904-1973

the flies forage again, *las moscas sanguinarias,*
banishing, barbering, lengthening skirts, executing,
gangrening the long sweet land

father miguel died in the hospital too, pablo,
in valparaiso, after arrest, interrogation,
the unction drying on his swollen mouth

and juan alcina was found, outside santiago,
without identification, submerged by the 10 holes in his chest
running blood in the mapocho river

and your library sacked by the robots,
last payment for singing long, and dissonant
to the iron clubs, the lace-and-chalice cosmetologists,
        the well-trained in tyranny

oh pablo, next time, next time
in the blind air, non-elected we vote with bullets, terror,
next time pablo, next time
for juan, miguel, lechery, the scattered poems

RITE OF PASSAGE

my son
his football voice
louder than lions
wears no. 17

i see him break thru,
fading, into me,
shimmering in musculature
all fierce, hard joy

my wife weeps
at weddings
not games
far away her tears

she must allow me mine
on these sudden October fields

BETRAYAL

The Judas kiss is an archetype—all have tasted it. From Christ to Caesar, to you and me. Our memory of it is sharp, because in betrayal we are twice hurt. A wound is hard to bear. Add betrayal as its cause and the heart knots. Caesar struggles for life as the assassins stab at him. But when he sees his friend Brutus with a raised dagger his heart collapses within: "Et tu, Brute? Then fall, Caesar!"

Violation of trust is murder more painful than knives; the gentle kiss of duplicity more stunning than any blows. Bad enough to be delivered over but that we are turned over by the treachery of friends: that's the sting that scars our soul.

How can we deal with this experience? Can we grow through it? Some people don't. As a student minister in Vermont I knew two families that had nursed an embitterment against one another for 20 years. It had to do with some betrayal of love and properties.

Their resentment toward each other had finally encompassed themselves, neighbors, Church, God. Their whole universe of meaning was poisoned. Time does not always heal, I noted carefully in my work diary. There is danger in betrayal that we brood until anger becomes sullen, stuck, etched forever in the set of the jaw, lines on the face.

We must work against that. If we cannot forgive those who knifed us in the back (and who of us are saints?), we can at least look to our own welfare; and never give those who hurt us the satisfaction of mutating our warm blood to vinegar. So less respect for what they did at our back and more respect for what we can do for our future. We must move on to life.

A second lesson my Vermont families never learned. Not all we call betrayal is actually so. A foolish trust betrays us at times, not our enemies. Samson believed in Delilah, though three times in a row she proved unworthy of trust. That Samson let Delilah deceive him a fourth time doesn't mean he was betrayed. It means he was a damn fool.

In the pain of betrayal we understandably fail to take any responsibility. But it takes two to tango. The dance of deceit is a subtle duet. Othello moves with Iago, Antonio gambols with Shylock, Washington promotes Arnold, Caesar is forewarned, Jesus knows the motives of his men; and we have done enough hurting ourselves to recognize the capacity in others.

A third lesson. In our self-centeredness we often assume claims on others we have no right to. We think others owe us—duty, loyalty even generosity, when in fact they don't. We take others' gifts as if they were ours by right. Parents, children, and lovers are notorious in this conceit. We sue for debts never contracted for, except in our vain imaginings. Our sense of betrayal will diminish as our neurotic expectations of others decrease. We don't own each other.

Finally, as with people, so with life, with God. We shouldn't feel betrayed when we are refused what was never promised. Enough betrayals without concocting more! The cross is fair warning of what to expect in life. But don't bury it in virulent resentment like the families in Vermont, or try to smother it in the lilies of innocence. Those of us who have recovered know it won't work.

ALIENATION
AND ENGAGEMENT

Unfamiliar places and people and objects seem like toys to me. When I drive thru a new place or enter a strange town I find it hard to imagine that real life goes on in it. Nothing "tangibilitates." New faces appear as actors might, and buildings look like stage props. Even the graveyards come on like scenery. (It takes an Emily Dickinson to remind me that "this dust was once ladies and gentlemen.") For me unreality hovers over the unfamiliar, the unknown, the unloved.

I am more apt to speed thru a strange town than I am in my own neighborhood, more apt to be peremptory with strangers than with friends, more apt to be uncaring about the far away than with the close at hand. I'm always surprised, for example, when I bump into the reality of the "unreal": overhearing a waitress in a restaurant talking on the phone to her husband, hearing a baby cry, smelling food in a kitchen that I thought was a magazine ad, or meeting the parents of people I know, or touching the lives of persons whose realities I could never imagine from their faces in photo albums.

There's some advantage in keeping the world—its people and places—in the realm of the unreal. The sufferings of war on TV newscasts are unreal to me. The unreal does not cause me pain, I do not have to respond (be responsible). The mind can remain unconfused, the heart free from the burdens of engagement.

But keeping the world strange, out there, abstract, unknown, unreal, finally turns us into monsters. Something deep in us knows that to be fully human we must embrace our world, tangibilitate it—smell its smells, taste its wetness, overcome its unfamiliarity, enter its fullness, its pain, too.

Life is too wonderful to treat like a toy, a stage prop. The world must be known, to the edge of God. To be human we must risk again and again, in spite of the great cost, the mind and heart of our human love.

IF ONE MEMBER
SUFFERS.....

TV newscasts covered the escape and recapture of five desperados from the Federal prison in southern Illinois this week.

The recapture was exciting—police, vigilantes, dogs, helicopters, submachine guns. The men were caught, we gather, after a difficult night and day. They were separated, dazed, cold, hungry, thirsty, desperately thirsty. No one put up a fight. Each surrendered meekly.

It was important that these criminals were recaptured. I have only to imagine escaped killers, say from Walpole, stealing around my parsonage windows, to appreciate the protection of our law enforcement agencies.

So I don't wholly understand my reaction to the newscasts.

I was rooting for the escapees, wishing them well, hoping they'd get away—a boat to Rio, a cattle-car to Canada, a raft to the South Seas, that they'd get a new chance, to homestead, fall in love, farm in Vermont, ice-skate, watch the Red Sox, anything better than the grey lunacy of incarceration.

Why this irresponsible and irrepressible well-wishing for these five convicted rats? Why did I want them free? Many reasons I'm sure, beginning with what I've already indicated: my revulsion, psychological and deep, against prisons. I've visited dozens, from county jails to death rows, and I always leave every prison I go into feeling dirty and sick.

Other reasons for hoping the five would escape successfully? Admiration for any Houdini, any against-the-odds achievement. It was an "escape proof" prison. I have to salute. Is this part of an ancient protest against the Invincible System? Rooting for the individual over the group, the single one against the bureaucracies, man against the state?

The move from bondage to freedom is a fundamental motif in human history, maybe all of life. Breaking the yoke of bondage is the first and basic story of the founding of religions and nations. It is mythic. I think we quicken to any escape story, in the marrow of our muscles.

Another reason: we spend billions in spying, assassination plots, subversion of foreign governments, manufacturing new poisons, paying agencies to violate law and human rights—and we don't unleash dogs on them. If any man in America should be in a federal penitentiary for crimes against God and country it is Richard Nixon. Yet he lives in luxury, pensioned at $60,000 plus with your tax money and mine. I wanted those five desperados to escape as a way, however perverse, to balance the bent scales of American justice.

But the biggest reason was the TV photos of those criminals, and the reports of their asking for a glass of water at farmhouses. The faces of those men, not surprisingly, were haunted, lonely, human, mine.

SWEET JESUS NO

The famous pictures of Christ by Sallman that you see for sale in drug stores and brummagem art galleries are without any redeeming social value. Jesus is painted as a religious Kewpie Doll, a tender fag with a penchant for sheep. The depictions are fundamentally obscene and anti-religious.

At the same time they are an unerring reflection of the blasphemy of pietism: the imprisonment of the gospel into purely personal terms, the domestication of the infinite into conforting categories, the trivialization of the portentous, the tragic, the powerful, into soft pools of narcissism and sentimentality.

These obscene pictures have attracted the prurient interest of Christendom, as they hang in pastors' studies and church parlors across the land. The titillating message of Christ is: "Be pleasant, be pleasing, be content, be passive, be modest, be sweet." And so the Church has been seduced into historical irrelevancy and the great prophet of Nazareth reduced to a sycophant and servant of middle class comfort and the status quo.

I would remind you, especially during holy week, of the lies in that picture of Christ. You must know that the last week of Jesus had nothing to do with passivity, sweetness, "personal" religion or peace of mind. It was a week of shouting mobs, marching soldiers, argument and diatribe, whip cracks in the temple, smashed bankers' tables, threats, charges, trials; a week of betrayal and blood, a last supper with friends, a hymn sung together, and then darkness and the shaking of the foundations of a whole civilization.

I do not urge the suppression or censorship of Sallman's portrayals of Christ which are obscene and phony. I only urge we not buy them. The renewal of the Church and other redeeming social values are at stake.

ON THE
CELEBRATION OF LIFE

No one is against the celebration of life. And that is the theological trouble with this bromide. Charles Manson believed in the celebration of life. So did Hitler. Life per se is an ambiguous good. It's not whatcha got but whatcha do with whatcha got. Religion is more than a mindless jumping up and down about how super it is to be alive. I do not celebrate life when I pray at the graveside of a young mother or wait through with the despair of a family in a hospital emergency room. Celebration of life? How inaccurate, unfeeling, even blasphemous. You don't uncork champagne and shout hellelujah for life all the time. Sometimes you just try to endure it, in pain. Mature religion reminds us of an ethical dimension and a tragic dimension which the phrase "celebration of life" does not contain. Commitment to a *way* of life and the capacity to *endure* what life does to us are surely as crucial as expressing our jollity at the ambiguous vitalities about us and within.

SINE NOMINE

Occasionally, our command of English is best shown by silence.

PRAYER AT NEW YEAR

I send no wish to the Impossible
Or prayer to Maybe, Perhaps,
No promise birthing pretense, despair,
Or longing that sighs like a wrack.

In a world mad with our choosing
The warfare this year will glare,
And mornings will turn to darkness
And most will be worse for the wear.

So I wish you simply endurance,
Luck among the mines and snares,
Respite for some shining at table,
Less pain than you're able to bear.

With this an occasional glance
Into other's eyes that care,
A minimum of broken lances
And a heart still able to swear.

PRAYER AT EASTER
(FOR A.C.S)

Lord God of Easter and infrequent Spring,
Thaw our wintry hearts.
Announce the large covenant to deceitful lands
Drive the sweet liquor through our parched veins.
Stir the vacant eyes with green explosions
    and gold in azure sky.
Smite the pall of death that hangs like desire,
Lure us to fresh schemes of life.
Rouse us from tiredness, self-pity,
Whet us for use,
Fire us with good passion,
Rekindle thy Church.
Restore in us the love of living,
Bind us to fear and hope again.
      As we thank with brief thanksgiving
      Whatever odds may be,
      That life goes on living,
      That the dead rise up ever,
      That even the weariest river
      Winds back to springs under sea.

Both,
Both,
My
Girl

TWENTY YEARS
IN THE MINISTRY

Twenty years ago I began reading articles by ministers and theologians on "How My Mind Has Changed in the Last Twenty Years." In these articles, boiler plate used by religious editors on off months, the minister always:

1) expresses astonishment that twenty years could have gone by so fast, followed by a minor peroration on how it is to be hoped that we will all take advantage of however much more time, in God's mercy, we are granted;

2) confesses, in the face of the last decades of planetary convulsion that he is a wiser and deeper man, less grandiose in expectation, less naive about the difficulties standing in the way of human fulfillment; and

3) that, given the above, he is surprised by the prescience and perspicuity of his earlier youthful insights and more than ever convinced of their fundamental soundness and relevance for the contemporary situation.

This type of article brings out our stockiest of stock responses. It also presents an unrivalled opportunity for the display of intellectual pride, unchecked by any guardians but our own self interest and enfeebled memories. I decided twenty years ago that I would not indulge myself in such nostalgia and prevarication.

Beyond that I figured it quite unlikely that I'd ever complete the twenty-year period required for this generational genre club. I supposed that I'd simply flourish in the vigor of my fourth or fifth year in the ministry as a bright and perpetually promising young man, somewhat like a humming bird in stationary flights, forever winging before the flowers of summer.

Or else I'd imagine an early martyrdom, not the painful kind, but one rather symphonic and delicious, with thousands of mourners. And my enemies caught in a terrible grief, combining both jealousy and guilt, an unbearable torture, I surmised, which they thoroughly deserved and which I was not helpless to relieve, being in heaven.

Well, the hummingbird idea didn't hold up and my hopes for a yummy martyrdom have gone unrequited. And, as the articles say, I am astonished that twenty years could have gone by so quickly. It's almost twenty years now that my alma mater and denomination licensed me to pray on congregations and save the world. Let me say that while I am a wiser and deeper man, I am impressed by the fundamental soundness of some of my youthful insights. I urge them upon you for their relevance to the contemporary situation, etc.

What has changed in me over the past twenty years is not so much my mind as my whole organism.

I used to be a night person. Now I am a morning person. Twenty years ago I felt that life really began after sundown. I recall a professor's porch in Chicago, how a group of us argued and wrestled with ideas all night, how the sun came in on us in the morning as an insult, an intrusion. The days were but warm-ups. The torrid act of living waited for the night. Now nights are for sleeping and morning is the blessed hour, for work, for music, for walk and talk, to give thanks for the sun, to touch the palpable light.

I used to love football so much I could not bear to watch it being played without me. I now fall asleep during the Super Bowl and would much rather play handball or tennis.

Autumn was my favorite season. Now Spring is. I wait for forsythia more than melons. While we are on seasons let me move to the liturgical calendar to say that Christmas and birth was the greatest, now it is Easter and resurrection.

Twenty years ago I longed to traverse all the world's religions. Today there is barely time to explore my Jewishness and Christian-ness.

I was a Jeffersonian liberal for enlightened capitalism. Now I am a left-wing socialist for regional autonomy.

Twenty years ago I explored the vast generalities. Now I would like to have my own garden and make small poems.

These are some of the changes that have overtaken me in the past twenty years. Let me conclude by saying that it is to be hoped that all of us will take advantage of however much more time God in his mercy grants us, to enjoy the forsythia and save our world.

THE THEOLOGY
OF TV COMMERCIALS

TV commercials are getting more openly theological these days. Their appeal is explicity religious.

Polaroid promises to halt time, preserve meaning and hold it eternally on a 3x5 celluloid. Now you and your loved ones can laugh at the passing flux. A flick of the finger and your likeness ascends to where moth and rust do not consume. (Immortality, however, is not instant. You still must count to ten.)

State Farm projects the archetypal Good Samaritan. Your're safe in their everlasting arms, or hands. A soprano chorus of angelic religiosity sings of State Farm's 24-hour-a-day Good Neighborliness. They also fix your child's bike chain on their way to the office. That you pay $82.20 premiums every quarter is ignored in their commercial. But then it's glossed over in the Bible account too. (You don't believe that guy on the Jericho road gave all that first-aid, donkey ride and carte blanche at the hotel for nothing, do you?)

Should you suffer in 1973 from anxiety attacks then what you might need is a Piece of the True Rock. No more sleepless nights worrying if your house is built on sand. Let the wind blow and the flood beat. With this piece of the Rock you can have the geology of the cosmos on your side. Life up your eyes unto it, and go to sleep.

But Schlitz is best of all. The get right to the basic religious question, How can I be saved? Answer: live with gusto on a 75 ft. schooner with an ice-box full of Schlitz. (Don't run out, because there is no salvation outside Schlitz.)

Seize the day. Salvation is not by grace, but by grabbing. Remember—and here is their basic theological point, you only go through once in life, so grab while the grabbing's good. Schlitz theologians (often referred to as the Milwaukee School) argued this point for months, about going through only once. The argument finally resolved when their religious sociology research team reported in that Americans who believe in reincarnation are statistically insignificant and given to wine bibbling.

So, if you ever feel anxious, mortal, lonely, depressed, insecure, unsaved, take my advice: grab your Poloroid, pay a premium on Gibralter, and guzzle Schlitz. No more fear and trembling, no more dark nights of the soul. Do these things I have said unto you, and for that perfect peace, passing understanding, take Rollaids.

REMOVE MY NAME

Once in a great while you get a letter like this: "Remove my name from your mailing list. I refuse to have Communist pamphlets come to my house or anti-Christ leaflets which your newsletter certainly is if I ever saw it. Teaching so-called sexuality and mixing politics with religion! My ancestor framed the Constitution to take care of people like you. Too bad it didn't. What's happened to plain old fashion religion I'd like to know. We kept sex in its place and worshipped God not permissivism. No wonder the world is rotten with churches like mine taken over by the likes of you. I won't support it any longer. Though it still has great sentimental value I've had it with socialism and sex and your fuzzy radicals."

Usually you answer this way: "Thank you for your frank and honest letter. I am saddened and disturbed by the lack of communication among us that could eventuate in such a lack of communication. For any part I've had in the failure of the communication process, let me apologize, for myself, and on behalf of the Church. It is obvious that we have failed you, for which I am most sorry. Your lifelong membership here is a valued asset to us all and we are proud as you are of your colonial heritage which we've heard so much about over the years. Please reconsider your decision to resign from the Church of your fathers (and mothers). We need your vigorous voice, and yes, even your hearty occasional dissent. That is what a democratic Church is all about. I'd like to meet with you soon to discuss the very complicated issues you raise about sex and politics in Church. I certainly respect your right (if not *all* the conclusions you reach) to register dissent. Like a family that sometimes quarrels, it doesn't means we aren't still a family. Please stay on to give us the continued support of your witness and wisdom and wit (if I may interpret some of your sharp comments as such). You may have been "gruff" and a little "crusty" but I thank you for your letter and love and concern for the good of the Church out of which it grew."

Once in a while though, there's a temptation to answer like this: "We are delighted to get your name off the mailing list. Besides costing us money it's been stinking up the reputation of this Church for forty years. Your support of the Church, I just learned from the treasurer, is unrecorded for forty years, though we keep hearing about your generous offerings. We're thinking of talking about it with IRS. Your letter has gone to the pathology lab. You come on like a Neanderthal, a troglodyte. If your ancestor helped frame the Constitution (which I doubt) he's rolling in his grave in shame for siring a descendent like you. You have nothing against politics in the Church as long as they are your politics—primitive, prejudiced and puerile. Your obsessive comments on sex are sick. This Sunday I will denounce your kind from my pulpit and spell out why people like you are worse than Benedict Arnold, or Judas Iscariot. Any more letters like your last one we're turning over to the health department. Phew, good riddance. And God bless you."

THE LIBERAL CHURCH

This place is the liberal church:

A place to go where you know you belong—

Where the mind is free to soar beyond the coercions and crudities that inevitably beset all orthodixies;

Where the heart is free to extend that larger love to all, unencumbered by dogma, tradition, race, country or class;

Where the hands are free to work for the cause and the hope of peace;

Where the soul is free to open, stretch, discover, develop, deepen, change and grow, always and continuously and progressively;

Where the rights of individual conscience and action are guarded with vigilance, out of belief in the fitness of diversity, the liberty to be different, out of "eternal hostility against every form of tyranny over the mind of man";

Where the glory resident and potential on our planet earth is enjoyed and celebrated, not denied or blasphemed in the name of sin or spurious escapes to another world;

Where the promise of humankind is nurtured, supported and blessed, and never cursed, degraded, or despaired of;

Where the faiths by which we live are regarded as important enough to be examined and checked against the tests of experience, the canons of logic, the methods of science;

Where the church is committed to speak and act on the great moral issues of the day, not denying or hiding or ignoring its prophetic role as an agent for the transformation of society into a kingdom of righteousness;

Where the whole person can enter fully into the religious mood without insult to his reason or irrelevance to his daily life;

Where the whole person can utilize, without reservation or cant, the resources of his own tradition, whatever his particular religious heritage is;

Where people are invited to be themselves—in joy, in sorrow, in the struggle of the deeper self to be born, in the resolution of some great issue, in the witnessing to high ideals, in living and dying, seeking and finding and serving—

A place to learn, to grow, to sing, to stand;

A place to be a more authentic self;

A place to encounter, reckon, judge, accept, and be accepted;

A place to be challenged by new insight and be reminded of what one already knows;

A place to respond to a vision of holiness, all arts, and other depths;

A place to be with others in co-creating with God;

A place to provide conditions for the coursing of the Creativity which vivifies, heals, and makes all things new;

A place to go where you know you belong—this is the liberal church.

THEODORE PARKER FERRIS

Theodore Parker Ferris, age 63, died Nov. 26. He was 30 years rector of Boston's Trinity Church and the best preacher I ever heard. Along with 1,600 others, I was at his funeral last Wednesday noon.

It seemed surprising that Ferris was not standing alive and vibrant in his old pulpit, that instead his body lay coffined in the chancel. I imagined him only asleep on that bier, that momentarily he would lift the pall and be up and about conducting services. Such conjurings rise easily in the hours of early grief.

Few preachers I've heard could touch him. Perhaps Reinhold Niebuhr, Howard Thurman, Fosdick, King, Wally Robbins, Waldemar Argow of Baltimore. The gift is rare. Ferris had it in abundance—the gift, the magic, the charisma.

The work "Charisma" first appears in western literature in the 6th Book of the Odyssey. To help shipwrecked and begrimed Odysseus to win the favor of the people on whose shore he'd been cast, Pallas Athena, daughter of Zeus, laid on him a grace, a special favor, a bright shimmering quality that made him, in spite of his bedraggled appearance, powerfully attractive, mysteriously alluring.

Well, Theodore Parker Ferris from Pallas Thena, God, or someone had this gift laid on him. He stood tall but homely, with a long pale face, small eyes, thick glasses. He was formal to a fault and showed that slight effeminacy and fastidiousness that sometime overtake long-term bachelors. His voice was clear but not extraordinary. He was not a dramatic preacher, in either the best or worst sense. But he had the charisma.

To ask the secret of his great preaching is finally to ask a foolish question. If the answer were known our theological schools (and all other schools) would be turning out speakers like him on an assembly line.

Yet I would not indulge in mystery mongering. His strengths can be pointed to:

1—he spoke with the genius of simplicity, the kind that makes you say "Why, anyone could have said that." Yeah, try it.

2—he spoke to persons and out of their deep concerns. And so the weekly miracle, his hearers almost gasping, "Why, he's speaking right to me! How does he know?"

3—he spoke as a relaxed and forgiven man. He took himself and other people where they were, not where he or they thought they ought to be. The result was disarming, confirming. You never heard unintended anger in his voice (the one disturbing note I hear again and again in Unitarian-Universalist preaching).

4—he understood with Parmenides, who lived before Jesus, a doctine of the Incarnation. How is Truth revealed? Said Parmenides, "By choosing the right word." Ferris could do that, choose the right word. His language was revelational. He illustrated every idea, clothed every abstraction in colorful garment. If he dealt with the concept of power then he illuminated a volcano, live, erupting. If he spoke of God's glory, he'd describe Boston Garden in spring and tell of the sun hitting the gold dome of the statehouse at noon.

I once heard him on the problem of evil. He pictured a rosebush he had planted and how one morning he'd found it uprooted and torn apart, the senseless work of a hoodlum. He expressed his dismay and, later on, his need and commitment to plant in the same place another rosebush. That sermon, that rosebush, remain with me. That's 17 years ago. That's what is meant by memorable preaching.

Ferris's ministry, like all ministries, was imperfect. He lacked the prophetic courage of his 19th century namesake. He was no Amos. I doubt if any prophet ever sat, as Ferris did, as a Trustee of the Boston Symphony Orchestra. Sadly, I often heard him trim to the melody of viols and harps, away from the cataracts of controversy and the demands of social justice. The political allegiance of the non-controversial, "non-political" churchman is explicit and profound: it is to the present order, the powers that be, the status quo.

Against this I must say that at his funeral I saw two hippies weeping, and a tough militant-looking black barely containing his grief. I suspect Ferris did his best prophetic work, like many other embourgeoised clergy, on the sly.

He did send out week after week, year after year, a lively and healing and enabling word to thousands of people from all walks of life. Though a spellbinder, it was obvious that his concern was for more than the display of his own talents. He belonged to something prodigious, far greater than himself.

Sometimes when I think the preaching art has fallen so low that the poor crittur should be taken off behind the barn and mercifully shot, I am reminded, as I was last week, of what the pulpit, under grace, can be. Theodore Parker Ferris, in spite of the pietism that begrimed him, was a window to a splendor beyond our devising. He preached in light. His tongue was a fire.

OPEN LETTER SURGERY

To the Powers-That-Be
South Shore Hospital
South Weymouth, Mass.

Dear Madams or Sirs,

My son Garde and I visited you one morning last week, to check the cast on his arm. While waiting we talked about hospitals, their history, how important they are, and what it means to be dedicated to health and healing.

This letter grows out of our conversation. We noted that 10 paces from the Admitting Office and 10 paces from the entrance to the Emergency Room glistens your handsome Cigarette vending machine. It's the largest and classiest I've seen, advertising 20 colorful brands. The glass gleams, the chrome sparkles, like a fine piece of medical equipment you'd find in your operating rooms, say an oxygen machine to help a patient breathe while you remove a lung or two.

Do you catch the irony?

Do Weymouth police sell burgler tools? Is avocado with mayonnaise on the menu at Weight Watchers? Does the local fire station vend Roman candles or skyrockets? Do our drug stores have machines where you can pull a lever and pick out the disease of your choice?

I know that preventive medicine is still looked upon as subversive by those enterprisers who see health not as a responsibility but as a business means to private wealth. But I find it incongruous that our hospital should openly *permit* and *promote*—both words are carefully chosen—the pushing of a habit denounced by every health organization on the planet as a menace and hazard.

How can I get across to you? I meditated about it with my son. "Hey, dad, tell them that having cigarettes here is like having a submarine with screen doors."

I said OK, I'll tell them that. It may be too subtle, but I'll tell them anyway.

Yours truly,

TRUTH SERUM
BITES CLERGY

All ministers are trained during their first years in the parish to start the fall with the announcement that they are overjoyed ("utterly thrilled" is even better) to be back at work after their vacations. The sin of pleasure is mitigated if one can confess how good it is to be away from it. So the fall word is, "Vacations are necessary, alas, for one's health and perspective, but how grand to get back into harness after those weeks of sailing and sleeping and reading and loafing and swimming and puttering and gardening and playing and doing nothing."

In, say a Texas newsletter, you'll read: 'Though the orchard acreage in New Hampshire is green and pleasant, I can't wait for the harness and blasting sun of our struggling fellowship on the wind-whipped plains of Oilville."

Or from a clergyman returning from sabbatical in London or the South Seas: "Yes, it was a grand experience in _____ (fill in) but it can't compare with _____ (fill in present location). How good to hear the phone ring during supper at the parsonage after all those sombre hours in the Bristish Museum! How pleasant the violence in the church school after the dusty carrels at Oxford!"

Many of our ministers sail. In the fall you unravel nautical knots like: "Sailing my ketch is fine for a season, but no joyous beating against the wind can compare with those fall planning sessions" (when deacon Smith makes his annual suggestion that we lower boom on the minister's salary. Or when Smith for the good of the Church, talks it up about the parsonage lawn and the skirt length of the Reverend's wife).

Walking across a bridge in Maine this summer a mean troll injected me with a serum and forces me to say: I'd like to be on the beach in Maine right now, not in my office in South Weymouth. I want to deliver some sermons, but I'd prefer it if you'd drive up to Ferry Beach to hear them. I'll call you when I'm ready. I'm glad to see people I love again, but I could hold off until Thanksgiving if I had to. Work is good for the soul and gives meaning to life. However, I'd like to think about that awhile longer on my strolls to the beach and tennis court.

Of course I'm fooling about the troll and the truth serum. How utterly thrilled I am, to be back, to take up the challenges, how ready I am to plunge into the activities, restored, eager, chafing at the bit. Ferry Beach was a grand experience but it can't compare with....

And if any of you are feeling guilty for not being more enthusiastic about taking up your fall schedules, drop by my tent, excuse me, my office, and I'll see what I can do to forgive you.

TEETOTALER

A favorite story of mine concerns the doctor advising his patient: "You're in bad shape," the doc says, "too much carousing—no more wine, women and song for you." The patient resolves to reform and comes back later to report on his success. "Did you follow my orders?" asks the physician. "Well, pretty well," replies the patient, "I cut out singing completely."

One song I remember we students sang thru theological school, in loud tenor range, was "Cigareets and whusky and wild wild wimmin they'll drive you krazy they'll drive you insane." There's a similar joke on this song, a variation of the doctor-patient one, about only taking up with ladies who've been calmed down. But I digress, or at least make prefaces, very chauvinist at that. Ah well, I'm lucky all women are so inately forgiving. Aaaagggghhhhhh!!!

The preface is that on January 10, 1967 after being a two-pack-a-day-man for 15 years, I quit smoking. I'm still pleased, proud, and slightly mystified by that virtuous resolve and the relative ease by which it was put into effect and kept.

And now, as of January 1, 1974 I am further pleased, proud, and again slightly mystified to announce that I am a non-drinker. Booze has served as a pleasurable friend to me for 25 years so my goodbye to it is a fond farewell. But at middle-age, for reasons of diet, health, money, personal ethics and the desire to stay awake at night to read more books, booze and I are parting.

My pleasure with drink over the years has been qualified, of course, by occasional hangovers, the impossibility for me of dieting and drinking at the same time, and the sad knowledge of parishoners and friends whose lives have been hurt or devastated by booze. Alcoholism ain't funny.

A colleague, who told me he and his wife once quit for a year, says the biggest hassle they had was with friends who kept trying to pour it on them; and how at some parties when costly and attractive drinks were lavished on guests, he and his wife couldn't even scrounge up a glass of stale fruit juice.

I haven't had that problem yet. At the social events I've tested so far, our hosts have been considerate of non-drinkers. And who are the non-drinkers? I worried about this, for I've tacitly agreed with Gen. Patton for years. He said, "I don't trust men who don't drink." Are they all overly-controlled, judgmental, lacking in wit, willingness to risk? Well, praise be, I learned last week that Woody Allen, the comedian, drinks Mai-Tais without the rum when he dines at Trader Vics. That's good enough company for me.

But I will not send drinkers to my back porch as I do my smoking friends. Alcoholic fumes, my doctor says, are harmless to the lungs of bystanders. Besides, I make the best martini in the world and it would be a sin to let a talent like that go unused. My guests will still enjoy that first zingy zonk of my superb martinis, that zonk which would convince Icarus himself to rev up his motors and give it another try. Meantime, I'll stick to the earth and secretly confess that one of the secrets of my martinis anyway is my *personally* stuffed anchovy olives (washed off in cognac to remove the Spanish fascist grease.) Nobody can match them.

The porter in Macbeth (Act II, sc. iii) descants on the equivocal character of drink, how it makes a man stand to and not stand to. I've never had a problem like that. And the only way I'd take up booze again is if I ever should develop any problem like that as a result of my conversion to teetotalerism.

So join me in three cheers, or rather two, to women and song. And another cheer to books, work, play, great causes, good friends and all other means healthy and non-caloric of transcending what Sylvia Plath has called the incalculable malice of every day.

Prosit!

NIXON

No, I will not let Nixon alone. The issue is too solemn. We have a president who has systematically attempted to overthrow one of mankind's greatest experiments in government in the history of the planet. Yet he is still free, powerful, at large among us, the head of the most immoral, corrupt and deceitful administration in the history of our nation.

His message to us, to our children, is clear: it is all right to lie, cheat, steal, bomb, murder, forge, burglarize, kidnap, deceive, usurp, spy, as long as you do it for the good of your country. There is no higher law. National security justifies anything, *and the president* decides when national security is involved. In short he is above law, free to create a secret police force, free to lie to the nation, free to suppress dissent, free, yes, even to bug his brother's telephone. Our president is not committed to democracy. He is committed to a political philosophy that exalts the nation above all else, and which regiments and suppresses opposition through the autocratic leadership of "one who knows best" what the people need. In short, Mr. Nixon is a fascist.

Gibbon in his *Decline and Fall of the Roman Empire* makes the chilling point that Caesarism (autocratic rule, fascism) came into the Roman Republic without any outward disturbance in the constitutional form of government. The Republic was still there, on paper. But its reality was gone, and we in America better take heed of Gibbon's warning. Weicker was right—we almost lost a country. We still may.

Will the Churches in America take any part in this mortal struggle being waged for the soul of our nation? Or are our churches so much a part of the problem that they will be no part of the solution? Is the split between politics and religion so complete, are we finally organized into such a state of irrelevance that the demonic forces of our time will be confronted and checked at last only by the unchurched and irreligious? Will the God of Righteousness finally say to us at a future date, "Go hang yourselves, good Churchpeople, we fought for America and you were not there".

I tremble, with Jefferson, when I consider that God is just. And I tremble for our churches. Too many years of nation worship, nature worship, peace-of-mind, personal growth and pious platitudes may have sapped us of our last prophetic concern for the salvation of the larger historical community. Nixon's values, alas, may well be our own.

After his conviction Agnew met the press. He spoke as an unrepentant and spiritually vicious man. But we must remember the company he keeps. Nixon wrote him, not in outrage for betraying the nation, but in regret and gratitude for his partner's years of service and patriotism to the country. This is the rottenness in our midst. A man lies and steals from the people for a decade, and he is thanked for his patriotism and service.

The distortion of language is now complete, complete as the distorted morality of our President. The American Civil Liberties Union is working on it. I hope they will be joined by our demonination and every Church in the land. Nixon must be impeached. He is public enemy number one.

KEEPING SANE
IN DECEMBER

I send out my annual warning against keeping Christmas, following good New England puritan custom of long ago. Perhaps it's a function of aging, a timidity born of depletion of energy reserves, but I believe the problem of keeping sane thru the December holidays cuts across age-group vitalities and calls for a new conservatism in the life-styles of most of us.

Below are 12 rules to be followed faithfully from now thru New Year's day:

1—Measure out your drinks in a jigger, and keep track of them, and no sloshing over the rim. You may not stay sober but at least you'll remember who's responsible.

2—Weigh in every morning, the greatest reality-check invented since flu or jail.

3—Read Euripides' *The Bacchae,* marvelous aversion-therapy for December disciples or frenzied celebration. (I won't give the plot away, but in one part at a party our hero, in a fit of glee, gets his arms torn out of their sockets by his jubilant mother, much to her later distress, and presumably his.)

4—Be a good listener for all your friends who will fall apart over the next few weeks.

5—When you wish people Merry Christmas and Happy New Year look them in the eye.

6—RSVP to December party invitations with a request for a raincheck in February, a month that needs all the help it can get.

7—Much of Xmas is a mass of cliches, best broken up by fresh collateral reading, for example, the New Testament accounts of the birth of Christ.

8—Avoid romantic entanglements during December. They are exhausting. And behind the clandestine candle-glow of the season's affair you will discover that your new saviour is as much a slob as your present husband or wife.

9—The next time you feel impossibly rushed, late with shopping, worried about money, gifts, sending cards, turn on and tune in Bach's Christmas Oratorio, lie back on the couch and disappoint the drug industry and Freudians everywhere.

10—Permit some Christmas lighting to go far into the night.

11—When I was a boy scout we were advised in the official manual to take cold hip baths to prevent sex from rearing its ugly head. It never worked, so I'm modest about offering counsel to those in inner turmoil, sexual or otherwise. But for those of you who get torn apart by holiday depressions or anxiety attacks, I commend long walks, looking at Christmas trees and then home for cocoa. Meantime we pray for shut-ins who can't walk out at Christmas and pray that they have devised other techniques for beating the devil, the holiday devil who has a genius for raising hell at the worst possible time.

12—And last, please don't feel too guilty about violating any of the above rules. Merry Christmas, Happy New Year, and a wink at a star in the night's dark sky.

THE NICEST GIFTS I EVER GOT

During this season of gift giving a good exercise is to make a list of the best gifts we ever got. That will tell us what is important, for ourselves and for people we want to give gifts to.

While I remember a Daniel Boone hat and a magician set with special affection, the nicest gifts I ever got are in quite another category: the carillonneur at Rockefeller Chapel who let me strike one of the largest tuned bells in the world during his playing of Ein Feste Burg; my mother giving me a complete Shakespeare for my 14th birthday; coach Al Terry saying "Little Wells, grab your bonnet," and permitting me to enter as a freshman into my first varsity football game; a beautiful lady on a ship when I was still an acned teenager who kissed my face all over and told me she thought I was handsome; Dr. Henry Nelson Wieman telling me he had thought for several hours about a question I had raised and responding with a written answer the next day in front of the whole class; night after night my father playing catch with me in the back yard until it got so dark we couldn't see the ball; a Unitarian minister in Kalamazoo who put his arm around me after my father died and kept it there a long time; a friend who flew several hundred miles to visit me when I was sick; a buddy who went to see three movies with me on the same day.

The nicest gifts people have given me have been enabling, confirming gifts, bestowing understanding and self-esteem, help in time of trouble and delight for ordinary days.

May I suggest that you, too, draw up your list of the nicest gifts you ever received. I think it will give some perspective on the kind of gifts we really want to give to others, this Christmas or anytime.

OBEDIENCE

I remember one time when I was a boy I found a dollar and I went downtown and bought three sodas, five Power Houses, and one issue each of *Batman, True Comics,* and *Terror.* I didn't get sick, I liked my literary investments, and I had an extraordinarily satisfying day.

Because I remember this it is not easy for me to moralize about the importance of inner discipline in the absence of exterior controls. In fact, I think this would be a much better world if more people felt free to drink three sodas if they wanted to, double dip.

However, there is something to be said for lima beans and vegetables. One of the facts of freedom is that we are given some choice in life about what it is we will be loyal to. We make decisions as to what and to whom we shall be answerable.

As children we are protected, guided, admonished, and compelled, to get enough sleep, to do our homework, to eat vegetables, to obey this rule, and do this and act thus. But in adult life there are really very few regulations imposed from the outside and they are quite rudimentary, e.g., do not shoot your neighbor or light fire to churches.

No judge or parent or policeman demands that a husband and wife should continually scheme to please one another. No law states that we must spur ourselves on to greater depth and integrity of personal existence, or else go to jail. No billy club is over our heads insisting on the fullest use of our highest powers. No criminal code threatens us if we choose not to respond to the hurt and estranged, or in doing our jobs well, or in being honest with ourselves, or in buying sodas for children. In fact, no one can demand of us much of anything that is humanely siginficant.

In the realm of adult conduct we are given wide latitude to monitor as we will. When parents, policemen and other compulsions are gone away, the test of maturity arrives—obedience to life's unenforceables.

ATHEISM

At last I have found a definition of atheism that makes sense. I can't remember where I saw it—maybe it was in Francis Bacon. At any rate the definition went like this: "A true atheist is one who handles holy things without feeling."

Now that gets to the core of the matter. An atheist is a person who is insensitive to the holy things of life and treats them accordingly.

Usually an atheist is said to be someone who doesn't believe in God. But that is very narrow and quite abstract. And it tells us nothing about the person who is said to be or claims to be an atheist.

What kind of God does he not believe in? An overgrown grandfather playing dice on Mt. Olympus or Sinai? Does he reject the notion of a cosmic boogy-man who frightens children, or of a metaphysical bell-boy who tends the needs of the faithful and accepts Sunday morning gratituties? Is the atheist opposed to the notion of God, or Gods (there are so many different gods people worship) drawn by analogy from the crudest images of the natural order?

If he does reject certain notions, images of God, that is no real sign of atheism. Far from it, it is the response of a critical and questing spirit who will not bow before the several idols of human invention. He is searching for a truth beyond them. And if this is the kind of atheist you are, welcome to our Church!

Unfortunately, not all atheists are of this kind. Especially when they are over 21. Chances are the run-of-the-mill atheist over 21 is fighting windmills, without Quixote's poignant justification.

Quixote handled all his life as holy and full of feeling, and when he attacked the windmills, it was out of love for the right and for the favor of his incomparable lady-fair, Dulcinea del Toboso.

The same cannot be said of the run-of-the-mill atheist. It doesn't take much imagination to attack the several shoddy notions about God. Something's wrong. Arrogance, insecurity, running too hard, flipness born of anguish, cultivated dullness, lack of feeling about holy things.

This kind of atheist is not on the track of truth. He's on the road to destruction. The former kind we want in our Church, the latter perhaps we can help. But he will have to put up with our custom of treating life as majestically holy, and our handling of it with religious feeling.

68

ANNE SEXTON'S SUICIDE

It was hard to shake off Anne Sexton's suicide this last week. The Pulitzer prize poet carbon-monoxided herself in the garage of her home in Weston on Friday. When I read her obituary in the *Globe* on Saturday morning my reaction was one of pique. I had just come in from tennis. The day was, you remember, a beautiful day, for playing tennis, watching football, picking apples, planting tulip bulbs, one of those New England mornings so close to perfection that you wouldn't ask for more.

Why, I asked myself, would a writer like Sexton, famous, well-off, pull a stunt like that when she could be alive on a morning like Saturday? She had books to write, friends to love, young poets to nurture, children to care for and gardens all over New England disclosing pumpkins so big and orange and absolute that you dare not look at them long for fear they'll whack your brain dizzy with astonishment for the next twenty years or more. She had so much life to come down on, and all the equipment to do it with.

But. Anne Sexton had had a long, long love affair with death. She had taken on a darker love. She blew it.

Dante wrote about suicides, in hell, caught in a deadly sin, the despairing, sullen ones who, says Dante, "in the sweet air gladdened by the sun keep within themselves the fumes of spite." Oh Anne, Anne, Anne.

In the ancient Church those who took their own lives, (that is those among them not demented, deprived of their reason and therefore their freedom), were forbidden burial in the graveyards of the faithful. Suicides, it was believed, threatened and betrayed the community of faith and must be laid to rest somewhere beyond it. As desertion in the face of the enemy is a mortal crime among soldiers (not for the running away, but for the threat to the flanks and the demoralization it exposes comrades to), so is the desertion of one's comrades in the community of life. We are all in mortal combat and have need of one another.

Unfortunately, Ms. Sexton's death will lure others in despair to imitate her cutting out. If they are poets it will increase their sales and readership. It always does. My final pique with Ms. Sexton that Saturday morning found company with James Dickey's criticism of the confessional school of poetry to which Sexton belonged. He had referred to it with malice and accuracy—as "the school of gabby agony."

This judgment stayed with me throughout most of Saturday but by evening time my non-Aquinian Calvinism began to reassert itself and I sensed that my anger with Ms. Sexton had more to do with the fall wind than it did with her morality. Wm. Stafford, another outstanding poet, put it precisely:

> Pods of summer crowd around the door;
> I take them in the autumn of my hands.
> Last night I heard the first cold wind outside;
> The wind blew soft, and yet I shiver twice;
> Once for thin walls, once for the sound of time.

And pique then turned to sorrow and sorrow to evening prayers, prayers for us all, the living and the dead. We cannot always ward off the great enemy. We tire. We run into bad luck. Who of us can measure the pain or the compulsions in another's mind? And who of us who have tasted depression as an unbearable beleaguring of spirit can stand in judgment over those who finally reach out for death as they would for a medicine.

Anne Sexton is not a favorite poet of mine (I agree with Dickey's critique) but I do confess my admiration for what she did. She did make it to forty-five. She did have a heart and brain full of fresh and authentic feelings. She did have the skill and patience to shape her experience into art. And she did have what I admire most in her, a courage, remarkable in any human being, but especially I think in a woman of our culture, the courage to permit the surfacing of deep and dangerous vitalities. May she now, now, rest in peace.

One of the gifts a suicide brings us, and that Anne Sexton brought to me thru my grief at her death this week, is the new chance to strengthen our own resolves to be as faithful as we can to the community of life that sustains us, and to do our best to support one another, hanging in there together, and seeing, now and again, with Eliot, besides life's boredom and horror, some of its glory.

DRAMA AT
FERRY BEACH

At Ferry Beach on the coast of Maine the days of sun can change to chill and gloom. At such vacation places for those in tents or trailers any rain or fog beyond the brief visits essential to the rhythms of life are quite unwelcome. Nothing, I have discovered, depresses a campground so deeply as the blotting out of the sun and the seepage of fog and rain.

For a brief while no one minds. The bad weather does not penetrate at once. The summer is young, smiles are bright: excursions to L.L. Bean's, antique stores, time for chess, talks with friends, that book to read. In the first evening chill the feel of cupped hands around a hot bowl of chowder is sensuous and the rain tapping on a canvass roof a benediction.

But not for long when you get socked in. The sound of the foghorn is a lamentation. Sleeping bags get heavy with dampness and there's no sun to toast them dry. Matches squish instead of strike, quarters that were large are suddenly cramped and crosswords become less than games. Boats are beached, gear gets soggy, men don't shave, you need goggles for tennis, wives overdrink, mosquitoes whir and children whine and the father who stuck with his company for twenty years to get this extra week wonders what the hell for. After a few days of the cold and damp the whole universe gets chilly. You think about packing and getting out. The once gold hot sands and the silver splendor overhead at night can barely be recalled.

On such a night in the late wit's end of our isolation and discomforts and waning vacations, it was decided, perhaps by instinct, by a few score tired, bone-wet campers to move by lantern and flashlight through the night and fog to Rowland Hall where with piano, chairs and stage we jerrybuilt a talent night. We gathered, a disconsolate congregation, for a show.

A first-time actor came onstage, a pillow in his sweater to make him hunchbacked, and recited from Richard III. He muffed his lines half way thru, itched his humped back, shook his head and departed shame-faced. To his surprise the applause carried him back, this time with the lines in his pocket which he'd take out and crib from whenever he needed to cue again. When he concluded and bowed, he did it to loud applause.

The show went on, with an odd magnification. Magicians who fooled no one got more oohs and aahs than Houdini, corny comics with corny jokes broke us up in laughter. The winter of discontent lifted, a spirit was loosed. A self-conscious little girl came with her Haydn to the piano. Her mother was with her to turn the pages. She looked nervous, judgmental, over-solicitous. The child looked dutiful, vacant, unsure, and too tender to show her resentment.

She performed, pitifully, miserably, with all the chagrin, unpromise and awkwardness of the human race. And when she finished it happened. The applause surged into a percussion of approval. Standing on chairs, stomping, shouting, whistling, we yelled our bravos and encores in a cacophony of joy.

71

When it subsided people went back to trailers and tents, our heads full of what I can only describe as hard, bright jewels. In the shared light of imagination around a human hearth we had bushwacked the damn fog and outwitted the night.

PARTY

Skull hazed, stumbling down steps
across the fog-filled lawn
he yields, staggered by trees,
piled leaves, around
the stone wall, december wet

shouts of "idiot," "bastard," stalk across
from the party and the cocktails,
unheard by him now

he struggles within the glue of dreams:
sees her face smile-covered in
        courteous disregard,
then moves onstage with unremembered lines,
then the football bus, going off without him
        though yelled at, pounded, helmet-banged
                now i lay me
                sigh me down

this road taken, or not, blundered by,
three marriages and a half
vows bare as spider bones stiffening
        on the night sky
songs from a nickelodeon in a gym
        crepe-looped long ago,
and all acts done, denied, forgiven,
                now i lay me
                now i

as children supine make angel-wings in snow
he strokes, burrows back to that first world
brooches of sun, lush curled caskets
                now i lay me
                lie me
                leave me down

the black mound exhales

(UNTITLED)

TYRINGTON—the dishwasher at Waldorfs didn't
make this morning's *Globe*. No velvet honors
draped his whitened back, no traveling fellow-
ships lured. His passport was barely to Suffolk
Downs. Tyrington had no library card, no
large notebooks. He read what a Krishna might
hand him. His publisher wasn't. Tyrington
used rope under a bleacher. He owned no car
or garage. Tyrington had worked Waldorfs for
a month, returning as best he could the smile
of the dwarf waitress who carried trays to his
hoists and steam in the shining stainless steel.

POEMS SHOULD WHAM NOT BE

come on, poem
flash
stun
like a Mack truck grill

when they near you
hit brutal
out, shatter, lacerate

alien other
drive them back
an armageddon of snails
slashed by laser

EPITHALAMION

the conjoining of poets
beyond passion's hour
is sufficiently rare to sing,
the mirrors of self quite blinding,

so for apollo's own to bind
themselves in ancient ritual, law
is so audacious, avant-garde
as to judge us all

we celebrate therefore
beyond this sweet riot and
new armory against dark
your quite remarkable triumph
over the narcissism of false art

WHY BLUE WON'T DO
(FOR YOU)

blue is the color of oxydol pellets,
baptish hymnals, tatoos, penny depressions,
the plaster cape on every marian statuette
blue is a sears & roebuck bathtub,
the undercoat of ever howard johnsons
blue talks too much
trains little boys queer
blue is julie andrews
blue won't screw

the best things in life are not blue
modigliani crotches
trees, sun,
egg foo young, ragout
eschew blue

blue is a snotty nose
a nasty beard
a stinking cheese
and they dropped dung on dover

so be true....
did it adieu
make it taboo
eschew blue too

SLANT RHYME ORGY
OR
PITCHED CREAM
AT THE HIPPOCRENE

Four poets with roots near Rome
Bowed and coupled to Orient rhyme.
When queried why they did
They parphonically pled
"We poets just love oblique reams."

As approximate pairings flamed
and dissonant halves arranged
A critic in his spleen
Keeled over in pain
And the poets off rhymed on his grave

YES, VIRGINIA

You'd know if Santa's a lie?
    Not just a melter in the snow?
Real as this fireplace, this creche, this thigh?
    Haunch by the log, drink our night's glow,
    I'll put you the argument made long ago,
Whether we're unsponsored, out of darkness sent,
    Or if we hear sleighbells beyond our woe,
And see reindeer, gifts, in this firmament.

Ah, few will argue yes anymore. We're shy
    And with pain. A lifetime's a blow
And much in our sky is bent awry.
    Little's left to assuredly know—
    Hallucinating is easy to show.
We huddle at hearths of small intent
    And hear no elves or Santa bestow,
Or see reindeer, gifts, in this firmament.

It's a shivering we modify
    On Decembers spinning below,
A trembling we pacify.
    A galloping heart sings slow
    When we open the rye to overflow,
Sing a gala sentiment,
    Sight a holy tableau,
And see reindeer, gifts, in this firmament.

Envoy

O stranger, to banish the hovering foe
    That shadows our ascent
We drink to December's overthrow,
    And see reindeer, gifts, in this firmament.

A COLOR

all breathe
in her grip
chromatic collusion's
oddest alchemy
ice and fire

fecund fuse
pushpullpushpullpushpull
venus calculus
lure of contrariety
until dying

and death returns to whiteness
no oddity
wherefore
is purple praised
ambiguous
tense, royal

UNIVERSITY
OF CHICAGO

This excellence funded on Marshall Fields and Rockefeller dust
Where the first Ferris wheel sparkled on nights of the 1894 Midway and is
    now permanently dismantled, under urine
Where by whose large carillon dumb scholars pass, glutinous to books, all 72
    soaring bells spurned by their cogito ergo airs
Where moon-lit strolls are taken if at all by chapters in Lit 301
Where faculties are united by a central heating plant and a grievance over
    parking; and students by dirty clothes, mid-west births and brains for lust
Where the hersey of clean fog only occasionally indentures the fake gothic thrusts
    of this damp establishment of smog
Where the greying mother, great by the Lake in which fish swim blind, stumbles
    on in conceit of mind, well-endowed
Whose last concession to sport was a nuclear fidgiting in an unused squash court
Whose most living art is an accurate reproduction of Nefertiti in the Oriental
    Institute
This testament to intellect unfleshed.
And in his mahogany room at the Faculty Club a visiting professor of ancients
    smiles at the oranges he smuggled on to campus

HOSPITAL CALLING
(FOR M.C.D.)

He picks up at the desk
five pale green cards at twilight
religious preference checked, vaguely

up echoing clean stairs
but at the third floor
he puffs to the elevator,
abdomen lurching
belching onion, gin

he numbers wings, corridors
doctors pass by, he smiles,
on their way to yachts

he returns also the smiles of nurses
their white asses
tooo a nimbus around his cock
rings of delirium

soon five rooms and a ward
settle
a chorus of gratitude in geriatrics
for his artifice of prayer
divine mint among aging smell
he leaves, rectory routed

twisted awake
neighbors say
it was a sigh
a moan a
no
no
they do concur
it was a wail

BOYLSTON AT TREMONT

At Wanda's you pay a hundred for kicks,
can tell they aren't sincere
here Boston coppess real, goddess cop
packs 38 does Judo hard, she'll hurt,
black holster curves on hip
thonged billy dangles down thigh so

Smash doors at Liberty Bank & Trust Co
Run across red-white sashes Smash Brigham's

Here she comes Ochrist, don't kneel
fight back, siren siren
bleed in her wagon
to station all cuffed

> The goddess cop shakes in anger
> as he ogles her terrible smile.

REUNION IN
SAN FRANCISCO

She knocks as the sun
garden of thighs
moist from taxis of this bay
to this high room over Geary
windows opened to trolley bells,
spider mums; down on this bed
her petalled clutch
over mouth and world and pain;
you are a kiosk, all flowerstalls
and these iris whose interior
pushed forth sons to flight,
the dark miracle,
we take again
the city sings in sun and light.

THE TRAGEDIES OF CLARENCE McDOUGAL

clarence mcdougal
caught his
thigamajig
in a cold casaba melon
and died in the ensuing draft

clarence's parents
attended the funeral
whispered reports
prevented any eulogy
the minister saying only
those who live by the casaba
shall......

most young americans
will keep their thigamajigs
out of the gold green
yummy slip/slip after that

"we're after the suppliers
the perverts who plant"
proclaimed the
chief of police

"O cockafuckledee"
sighed a melonolinguist
"you needn't perish at all
simply heat before serving
the yummy casaba"

.

II

clarence mcdougal
theological student
dropped used tea bags
on the heads of jesuits
strolling below

these efforts at sublimation
were, however, without effect

as clarence would
term after term
bump into a brass floor lamp
and find her erotic
or talking to the alto operator
drop the receiver into his lap
and come without paying a dime

clarence's later success as a
protestant divine
came to a shocking end
("jee-zus" he cried)
on his wife's night out
during an electrical storm
over his parsonage
where jesuits had planted
a purple princess phone
a curvaceous brass lamp
and an enormous amount of
ill will

III

clarence mcdougal
tuscan brute and dante buff
had her manlocked
but she knew
exactly
what to do

carefully
she placed
a cashew
on
her thigh

he went for it
got pincer-locked at the neck
and lectured at in heated rhyme

for his sexism
and vulnerability to peanut imagery

clarence at last cried
"i long in extrema
a switch to terza rime"
she complied
and clarence died
in a paroxsysm
of pudendal praise

leaving this
scratched behind
which she
discovered in her mirror
and sold to wormwood review
O
young poets
listen to my sigh
never dive for a cashew
on a lady poet's thigh
if you do
pray paradise she's nice
and
versatile in meter
to poets between her
yrs truly
r.i.p.
mcdougal

COITUS

(A Lucid Poem on Sexual Intercourse by a Poet Once Too Often Accused of
Confusing Syntax and Vagueness)

John[1] said to Mary[2]
You see this hard thing here?[3]
Mary said to John[4]
Yes, John, I think it's your dick.[5]
It's hard, Mary, sighed[6] John.
Why don't I insert it in my mouth,
purse my lips over it,
rotate my tongue around it,
move my head back and forth,
and suck it,[7] John? queried Mary.
Golly, Mary, and what may I offer in return
whose worth might counterpoise such a gift?[8]
Well, John,
you might
lick the clit
a bit
check the fit
we've a hit.[9]
So he did it.[10]
Then they engaged in a non-fuliginous act.
It was self-evident,
pellucid,
unmistakable,
what they were doing.
I won't describe it.
Some things are best left
to the imagination.
But let me frankly convey
it was a simple, straightforward
clear as glass
perfectly transparent
unopaque piece of ass.[11]

1 - heterosexual male, straight as God makes them.
2 - heterosexual female, likewise, though as a child she did overhear an adult
    conversation in which her third cousin spoke fondly of Krafft-Ebing.
3 - ambiguous perhaps, but the reader is assured the poet did not have in mind
    the odd hump on the back of John's skull.
4 - it is not unusual for people to respond when they see a good thing.
5 - a regional variant of "dong", vulgar for prick, cock, whang, peter, stick. In

Latin, penis erectus.

6 - the connotation here is of longing, desire, not, as Eliot avers, of ennui or weltschmerz.

7 - the "it" refers to John's rod, not, as has been argued by Eliot, (unconvincingly, one must say) a silver maltese cross that John might have worn, perhaps on Sundays. Eliot's thesis that we have here a case on intentional vagueness is simply unsupported by the text.

8 - drawn from Shakespeare, or someone quite like him. See the poet's article "Shakespeare No Queer" in the Dec. '72 issue of the *Lavender Nuts Quarterly*.

9 - Eliot sees here an analogue between certain liturgical movements of baseball and the Pomeranian Eucharest, northern rite, where the maltese cross, in a curious ambiance, is employed to impede ejaculation.

10 - "it" - not as syntactically elusive as Eliot would have us believe. To whit, it refers back to the clit, fit, hit, bit.

11 - "piece of ass." By a daring leap of metaphor, a synonym for screwing, balling, poontang.

HOLY

NO   MY

WOW   PLEEZE   GOD

STOP   JE-

OH   ZUS

YES

TRAINWRECK, ILLINOIS CENTRAL, SOUTHBOUND

Perhaps it's a student's book, underlined in red,
and a high I.Q. dripping over steel
that early morning sang goodbye
(withholding the intelligence of annihilation.)
His paper "Acts of Transcendence"
is scattered, footnoted before breakfast

Beside a nun, a full denial of God's communion
with this chaos of bursting arteries,
this track of terrible epiphany;
her pubic bone crushed in chrome,
her breasts wanton as a whore's laid waste,
her beads spitting a thousand protesting farewells

Toward this boy's arm jerking in vertigo waves,
a refugee clawing at bread,
a stumped witness to this wreck,
hinged moments earlier to a 12-year life
unhampered by glass and copper,
his limb persists, clawing, eerie

Near a blackman's wound spurting revelations
of all men who need no more hellos.
His spine roofed in advertisements, wires,
his mouth shows sausage, egg,
perhaps fries, salted wine
(I conjecture throughout this ruin)

Next to a woman's double damage.
Yes, she sounded joy at the doctor's disclosure
and with her man slid last night sanguine
around, her second pulse greeting.
Instead of cupping her sweetening milk
she bends her womb in iron rails

WITH APOLOGIES
TO RUPERT BROOKE

These things I have despised:
Carol Channing, February
tinfoil around a baked potato,
all car salesmen, gas logs,
sleeping bags wet, mosquitos, flies,
snails who drill into clams and suck them out,
shaking hands after losing six-love
cavities, Germans, opera, chapped crotch.

When time shall have blotted out all these,
sealed them under our common plot,
say only this of me:
he despised a lot.

ENDOWED LADIES AT THE WINDEMERE HOTEL, LAKE SHORE DRIVE, CHICAGO

Windemere ladies
Won't you come out today
Come out today
Come out today
Windemere ladies
Won't you come out today
And walk in the light of the sun

From lunches of cottage cheese
and harmless loops of pineapple
canes, walkers, tap, thump, back to suites
on the arms of black companions

After naps the elevators hum
descending ladies to porticos and tea
who discuss the heat, the chill, the cloud, the wind

The curling yellow hairs, still moist,
sprout between nose and lip,
powder falls, rouge from Paris sticks like cake

Waiting in the sun
to serve this wizened breath
the black busboy smiles at his ghosts and sisters,
moves like a jaguar,
flame over ice

Windemere ladies
Won't you come out today
Come out today
Come out today
Windemere ladies
Won't you come out today
And die in the light of the sun

THE GREATEST VEXING
FORCES THIS TRADE

In steam-fretted mirrors they see home,
these bathrobed men living at the Y
white skinned in sagging underwear
waiting with their pouches for a sink, a stall.
Rival shaving creams blend their odors
with a dozen flushes
cascading the public waste

They've lost their MGs,
gearing down into graveled drives,
the kitchen slung martinis
with a woman beyond courtings or cavils,
arm wrestlings with muscled boys,
notices taped to the refrigerator doors,
whose dental appointment, cat to vet,
Miranda's week to scrape.
They've lost the candled suppers,
slouching in front of TV,
giving the finger to Ford,
four pillows, dappled sheets,
the gifts of familiar terrain

for a hot plate with hash in the coils,
for the freedom to burn in a grey monk's cell,
for this slaughterhouse to bathe in.

Banquet Prayers,
Other Essays,
Poems

BANQUET PRAYERS

As a young minister I was in demand on the banquet prayer circuit. I offered Invocations and delivered Benedictions—to World Affairs Councils, sports banquets, testimonial dinners, cub scouts, political luncheons, for groups of fifty souls to two thousand. My prayers were well-liked; brief, pithy but sparkling, heritage-laden but au courant; and beautifully phrased, though I kept my artful craftmanship cunningly hid.

I specialized in ACLU and UN banquets, Fair Housing luncheons, and inter-racial affairs, but I'd intone for any group who'd invite me. I've given my jiffy prayers over conventions of bankers, horticulturalists, Friends of the Zoo, rock collectors, morticians.

It's not the ideal situation, these quick-charge, hit-and-run offerings, but it's no tougher than shouting parables from a hill. And if Jesus could compete with the hauling in of fishing nets and roar of the Galilean surf, I could—with the aid of a PA-system—do some good over the racket of waiters banging glasses and silverware at your average Cincinnati hotel banquet.

You have to be motivated. I was. We graduates of the Federated Theological Faculty of the University of Chicago figured we had a solid 15-year spiritual lead-time of the rest of the culture and we wanted to help people catch up. I've exposed a lot of folks to important bits of holiness, Chicago style, in my time.

When you're on the banquet circuit a few years you learn the ropes. You always meet a little competition, a Catholic priest, a Lutheran pastor, a Reform rabbi. You can get the jump on them by slipping in Isaiah, or St. Francis, or Luther during your prayer and thus one-up (or absorb) your colleague in ecumenical winsomeness.

Two distinguished clergy attend one banquet, like Alpha and Omega, to bless the assembled from both ends of the spectrum. All souls in between and the multitudes in front around their white-clothed tables get enveloped in religious feeling. We served as flankers for the Everlasting Arms.

I preferred Benedictions over Invocations, even though the crowd is then thinking about baby sitters and the tie-up at the elevators. You do pronounce the last word. Often the speaker needs to be corrected, or pummeled, usually for arrogance and self-righteousness. It was fortunate on innumerable occasions that I was on hand to show a better way, before the people went out into the night misled or imperfectly informed.

You meet famous people on the banquet prayer circuit, though there's a price-tag. I'd dash off to a formal banquet, tossing back to my wife, only half-facetiously, "John the Baptist had his hair shirt, I have my rented tux and cummerbund."

Now Vice President Humphrey acknowledges me. (It is customary for the main speaker to address the clergy at the speakers table.) He has glanced at his program and speaks my name like he's admired me for years. I acknowledge his greeting by a nod of the head, giving an indication of slight embarrassment over the formalities, and by a small circular hand movement inviting him to please-go-ahead-with-your-speech-and-don't-fuss-over-me. When you get this nod and hand gesture down right you can score very high on the humility scale. You have to do it fairly fast though or the speaker will go on without you.

Speaking of humility, I prayed really hard over Myrna Loy one time. Her then husband was speaking for Radio Free Europe and she sat next to me throughout the banquet. I knew as soon as I was introduced to her that I'd have to expand what I'd composed. Hundreds of people watched me chat with Miss Loy during dinner so I put on that Chicago School I-sit-next-to-famous-stars-every-day-look. I disliked what her husband said in his talk, what little I heard of it, for I was re-writing my benediction now to blast at his arrogance and self-righteousness. Meantime I lit Miss Loy's cigarettes and passed her more iced olives and celery than she needed.

Miss Loy has a rich, well-trained, melodious voice. You can imagine how moved I felt when she told me I had a nice voice too. I decided to help her, in two ways; 1) let her know, if not her husband, that the Church of God is not in the employ of NATO or Radio Free Europe or any other national idol; 2) that some of us choose to dedicate our talents, including our voices, not to the frivolities of the Hollywood amusement industry, but to the Lord God of Hosts, by God.

I waited at the podium after I had given a stunning benediction, hoping to see Miss Loy again. But she went off, probably against her will, with her rich husband and a cadre of reactionary big-wigs with pot bellies and wrinkled cummerbands.

I was reminded of all this last week when I got my first invitation in years to return to the banquet prayer circuit. Since my 15-year lead-time has run out, and because fame is short (my son asked me Who is Myrna Loy?) I declined.

But if you know any young minister who wants to learn the ropes about banquet praying (background, techniques, winning members by, practice and philosophy of) send him to me. I'd hate to see the art pass away or even degenerate into mere ritual.

GRAVEDIGGERS

I read by the papers that the gravediggers in New York City are on strike. They earn very little money so I am on their side. I recall the scores of occasions at gravesides on bitter cold days, following the committal, when families, funeral directors and I backed into warm black limousines to drive off, while the gravediggers, puffing cold, began their work of burial against the grey and icy sky.

Over the years and in better weather I have often lingered at gravesides to talk with these muddy-booted and death-toughened crews and I have developed a special affection for them. None is as humorous or carefree as Shakespeare would have you believe. It is hard work they do. No one is proud of them. In most cities they have not been able to form unions. I'm glad they have in New York. Reinhold Niebuhr, a famous theologian from there, used to tell his students, "The meek shall inherit the earth, but only if they organize." I salute my friends who deal with shovels, vaults, caskets, dirt and the dead amid the snow-covered tombs. I hope they win a decent wage, if not the respect of mankind.

FANTASIES OF AN UNEXPLOITED SAINT

The mail at Church generally consists of advertisements for steel chairs. Flyers arrive, impersonally addressed "To the Pastor." I open them. But my mind wanders and my eyes refocus as I imagine, now and then, reading....

Dear Rev.,

The market for sermon collections has been dead for years. But we smell a new wind and frankly want to be first—to publish *your* sermons! Don't worry about credits of plagiarism as we have a battery of lawyers standing by. See you at Locke-Obers on Tuesday with the Rockettes for the reception in your honor.

—Ed Darling, Beacon Buoy

Dear Clarke,

Rival factions agree on you as arbitrator, and will accept your judgments as final. Thanks for saving the UUA in all its endeavors which I'm endeavoring.

—"Punchy" West, Boston Common

Dear Rev. Wells,

You don't remember me but I remember you and the sermon 17 years ago that saved my life. Enclosed tickets for round-the-world trip. To ease that beautiful conscience of yours matching funds go to BAC and BAWA.

—Grateful Anonymous, El Dorado, Ohio

Dear Mr. Wells,

We at CBS know the importance of theology. Sevareid has lost touch. We ask you to take over with your own nightly commentary. And that's the way it is, ontologically speaking.

—Walter, NYC

Dear Dr. Wells,

Martial conflicts due to differences in religious backgrounds cause us to turn to you. The Christina will pick you up in Hingham Harbor any morning at your convenience.

—Jackie, at sea

Most Reverend,

Because of your understanding of Rome's agonies and the Pontiff's desire for fresh strategy, We pray for an audience. Madeiros in Boston will arrange flight. Kindly accept, under separate cover, the small El Greco as token of our Fatherly esteem.

—Paul VI, Vatican City

Dear Winner Wells,

Your motto "What's Good for God is Good for General Motors" takes first prize! We deliver the Cad convertible to Church Parsonage tomorrow. At your request the gold nameplate on the rosewood dash has been buffed dull so it won't be garish in the sun.

—Charlie Wilson Roche for the boys at GM

100

Dear Reverend,

To get right to the point, Reverend, we Patriots are having trouble filling our quarterback slot. If you'd be willing to "break loose from the cloth," so to speak, and help us out we'd sure appreciate it.

—Coach Mazar, Foxboro

Dear Reverend Mr. Wells,

I crave the infusion of a post-Barthian liberal sensibility, but not one innocent of Angst. I speak of Angst as dread before the abyss. My wife, a Unitarian, calls it, alas, "the shakes." She can't spell the word correctly and she pronounces it with a long "a," quite destroying thereby what little equanimity I have managed over the years to achieve. A certain inconsequential virtuosity begins to mar my work and I turn to you for counsel and, hopefully, collaboration. With my limitless descriptive powers and your intesticulating verve I sense new hope for American letters, combining, say, my Kierkegaardian weariness with your Emersonian oomph. May I call you soon?

—John Updike, North Sticky Surd, Mass.

A last letter invites me to the Weymouth Naval Air Base to be met by Air Force One. "While I want to make it perfectly clear that I am not now nor never have been a member of your denomination, some of my best..." I stop. Steel chairs refocus to interrupt the postal fantasies of this unexploited saint, and like them (the steel chairs) I begin to fold.

THE NEW ENGLAND
MENTALITY

What's different about New England from other places you've lived? It is different here?

First of all, no New Englander would ask such questions. It is assumed here that there is a reality west of the Alleghenies and that it is probably different. The question could come up only if you knew someone well, someone who was keenly interested in your background, who was also a regular reader of National Geographic.

But in response to old friends in the midwest, south, and on the west coast, here are some differences I've noted:

They have ponds in New England that are bigger than lakes where you come from. Ponds are lakes here. Tonic doesn't mean quinine water here. It is a general term for soft drinks. If you ordered a gin-and-tonic here you might get sick with grape pop poured in your gin. Falls are more spectacular here and winter skies are clearer. It can get cold, but it's not as grey and cloudy. Phone service is pitiful, though this is the only place in the country where operators don't ask you to spell U-n-i-t-a-r-i-a-n. There are more antique stores, auctions, barn sales per square mile than in the rest of the country combined. Hockey is a popular sport also.

In New England a driver will pull out of a driveway in front of you though he knows you are going 60 miles an hour. He doesn't think you should drive that fast so he risks his life and yours to make the point. In New England people drive through intersections and close their eyes and pray. But at those few intersections where there are traffic lights (Yes Virginia, there are traffic lights in New England) it is quite as dangerous as those intersections without them. There's a lot of religion at New England intersections. I met a minister in Weymouth last week. He asked me why there were no lights in Columbian Square. I said, "You're new here aren't you?" "How do you know?" he asked. He'll learn. Or die.

New England has Boston. San Francisco is the only other city in America that can touch it. People here mind their own business more, are less effusive. Sometimes it feels like coldness, at other times just dignity. It's not bad. In Dallas neighbors spill barbeque sauce all over your front porch and suitcases before you can unpack. And those friendly waitresses in Nashville who call you honey will belt you in the mouth if you follow through. If a New England lady calls you honey you know you got a pal.

They don't build apartments in New England. They build "apatments." They don't have harbors here, you go sailing in a "haba." And the word "Law," through some legerdermain of articulation I have yet to fathom, comes out "Lore."

A word about food: in New England you go to Whopper Burgers for hamburgers. (Only tourists go to Howard Johnsons.) But you don't say Whopper

Burger. You drop the "h" and the "er" in Whopper and the "r" and "er" in Burger, then combine the two into one word and say, as rapidly as you can, "Woppabuga."

Finally, dear friends from afar, I should tell you the woppabugas here are better than anyplace else in America. But, as a New Englander, I confess I'm not particularly interested in comparing ours to yours.

HERRING RUN
IN WEYMOUTH

On a chilly spring day last week, after school, the family drove to East Weymouth to see the herring run from Back River on their way up to Whitmans Pond. The herring were there by the score in a shallow pool in front of the bridge, readying themselves to negotiate the four wooden ladders beside the falls.

One of our boys looked around awhile, yawned, and went back to sit in the car, but the rest of us were entranced by the sight of the incredible ritual of Clupea herengus, this anadromous North Atlantic creature who honors us annually with a return to the home town after exotic adventures on the high seas. Quincy may care for the Adams family bones, Hingham may boast a 1681 church, Concord claim Thoreau, but how many towns in this world, and from Labrador to Long Island, can serve as alma mater to a herring run?

A few spectators gathered—some men leaning on the bridge rail, a troop of cub scouts with their den mother. The boys (no girls) climbed down to the ladders, lay on their bellies and with sleeves rolled up (never high enough) plunged their arms into the waters to grasp the aquatic vertebrates in their upward drive. Most could not be held for long, but every minute or so one of the lads, grinning with wicked achievement, pulled one out. All were between twelve and fifteen inches, beautifully colored, slim, vigorous, strong. I held one for a while, then tossed him up over the ladders.

The boys did that too; we hoped we were being helpful to the fish, to make up for the fun we were having with them. The cubs' den mother stood along the railing, admonishing her charges not to get wet and to be gentle with the fish. "They're full of eggs," she said. Only a den mother could think of something like that.

Nobody around could answer questions. Here is a miracle going on and you look around and all you can see are gas stations, a dry cleaning establishment, electric wires and the usual city crud. Where the fish come from, how many, how long they stay, how many they lay, what do they eat, how old do they get, where do they go, when, and why—some lore about this remarkable event should be posted or put on a plaque for people to see and read.

I noted a plaque in Cambridge last week. It commemorates the spot where the spreading chestnut tree stood by the village smithy. They remember an old chestnut tree. Surely we can give recognition of the lively heritage and mystery in our singular stream in Weymouth.

NANTUCKET ISLAND

My wife and I took a holiday to Nantucket last week. We left our two boys unattended for the first time. They insisted on it. I agreed it was the manly thing to do. After a yin-and-yang argument, Cora also consented.

We drove early on the 13th to catch the 10:30 ferry from Woods Hole. It was 12 above, sunny, cloudless. The drive down the Cape was bleak and beautiful. We had breakfast in Woods Hole and then boarded the Nantucket, newly renovated and much larger than the Uncatena. I read aloud to Cora chapters 14 and 15 from *Moby Dick*. We looked over the ship, yawned, had tea, walked the decks, and read from books I got from Tufts library about Nantucket.

I studied the Indian stories about how the island came to be. (All myths of origin are revelatory—Nantucket's has both humorous and tragic themes, a dialectic not unknown to any of us.) One is about an Indian who got sand in his feet and kicked his moccasin 30 miles out to sea. We all know the feeling. The other is of Indian parents canoeing after a giant bird who carried away their child in a deathly grip and dropped the bones at Nantucket and the fogs on the island mourn still. We all know the feeling.

Well, as Melville put it, "Nothing more happened on the passage worthy the mentioning; so, after a fine run, we safely arrived in Nantucket" at 1 p.m. We were met by friends and stayed in their 1790 house, across from the old Quaker meeting house. We drove the island (15 mi. x 2½), stopped at the moors, viewed the harbor from the Unitarian Church tower (where the town bell rings 52 times at 7, 12 and 9 each day), and walked up and down Main Street. Main Street in Nantucket is one of the most satisfying spacial enclosures I ever walked in.

We went to the Atheneum, the book store, the Starbuck mansions, the Jared Coffin House (full of Chippendale, Sheraton, American Federal, and tables and cabinets brought by whalemen from Japan and China). We took in Maria Mitchell, a famous lady astronomer, and, late at night, the Nantucket weekly paper, the *Inquirer and Mirror*. Like the weekly I grew up in, the front page contained the essentials: news of the fire department, patients at the hospital, the births, deaths and marriages, the steamship authority accepting a bid to lengthen the Uncatena, the tides in the harbor, an announcement from the Town nurse about German measles vaccine, and a proposal to raise the salary of the police chief from $9,000 to $9,900.

We celebrated my 41st birthday on Nantucket and had scallops from the bay and beach plum jelly. I share my birthdate with Schweitzer, Lindbergh and John Dillinger, but nobody on the Island was impressed.

Our hosts were wonderful, even to bringing morning tea to our bedroom, with a fresh geranium. One of them quoted in cockney an old saying, "Life ain't all you want, but it's all you got—so stick a geranium in your hat and be happy."

We sailed back to the mainland on the 14th on the 2:15 run, arriving home after dark, and sleepy. Speaking of that yin-and-yang discussion, the boys were fine, but I noticed every light in the house was on.

IDENTITY, IDENTITY, WHO'S GOT THE IDENTITY? OR BUTTONS, BUTTONS, WHO LOST THEIR BUTTONS?

A Chancel Drama "developed" in response to "voiced needs" from 25 Beacon Street telling us about a 15-month "process" to find out who we are. Or in 25's own electric officialese: "to focus the resources of our denomination to aid members of our congregations in achieving a clearer awareness and articulation of answers to the questions: What is a Unitarian-Universalist today?..." (Letters from 25 Beacon should be read fast. When read slowly they self-destruct on reaching the brain.)

SCENE: Command Room of Forward Group on edge of embattled forest. Ominous explosions and noises of chaos are heard all round. Plus cries of the untold for bread, for grace, for justice. Bulletins on catastrophe and impending holocaust along the entire front are scattered carelessly about the room.

SEC'Y (answering phone): Good morning, UUA! ... The leader? ... I'm sorry ... Not available ... He's having an identity crisis ... That's right, i-d-e-n-i-t-y ... He's tied up in a hammock ... like Richard Burton in "Night of the Iguana," ... No, they can't speak either ... Tied up ... Yes, the entire professional staff, top priority, major concern ... Yes, tied up in hammocks ... Like in the movie, groaning, teeth clenched, secretaries standing by ... You may think it voluptuous. We take it seriously.

CALLER (puzzled, astonished): You mean we elected you to squirm around in hammocks? ... At $30,000 a year? ... you're supposed to define goals, sell them, put them into action—to articulate identity, not groan about it ... You're confused!

SEC'Y: Not confused. Diffused.

CALLER: What's the difference?

SEC'Y: Lack of clarity in awareness of identity is more dignified. Everyone's confused. We've got identity problems.

CALLER: Let me talk to one of your bosses ... Pull his arm through the ropes ... Thanks ... I know it's highly irregular.

EXEC: Bad time to call ... I don't see any light at the end of the tunnel for at least 15 months ... Trying times, identitywise ... Of climateric proportion ... Several of us reaching that age ... Generativity vs. Stagnation ... Erik Erikson? ... What does he say? ... Get off your butt? ... That oversimplifies many facets of a very broad multi-dimensional problem.

CALLER: (pleading): Can't you do the Burton scene on your day off? At your own expense? ... That's right, a non-subsidized hangup ... Why tie up 238,136 Uni-Unis from 1,038 societies with you?

EXEC: We like company, fellow questers searchingly seeking their identities, avoiding premature closure, eyes always on the behind of the beyond beyond the beyond.

CALLER: We did *The Free Church in a Changing World* in 1963 ... Just the other day the Goals Committee Report ... You know our ages, incomes, politics, religious beliefs, sex preferences ... What more on our identity do you snoops want?

EXEC: That was yesterday. OM. OM.

CALLER: You should be negating frontiers and the crudest implications of history.

EXEC: Can't do everything.

CALLER: Look, untie yourself. Report for duty. There's not much time.

EXEC: Always time for programs of endeavor by participational processes to shed clarity on identity ... What's that? ... Same to you buddy ... You say we're paying $500 to be told who we are?

CALLER: Send it on. You've just been told.

EXEC (hand over phone, to sec'y): Oh, the insolence of non-office holders! Doesn't like our Identity Program.

CALLER: Identity is as identity does. He that seeketh his identity shall lose it. He that loses it shall find it.

EXEC (hanging up): What kind of nut would make a statement like that? ... Tie my arm back in the hammock will you dearie.

    (CURTAIN, with hammocks swinging existentially, a few whimpers and bangs, an ecological death rattle, and the sound of quite uncertain trumpets.)

TOWARD A
BIODEGRADABLE
THEOLOGY

Starr King, our theological school on the west coast, is in need this week of a bit of theological counsel. Their catalog arrived—beautifully done up, luscious, expensive, as fancy and costly as any academic catalog ever produced.

Typical. Starr King has lived on the brink of financial disaster for years—mortgaged properties, bankruptcy, last minute pull-outs, saved again and again by pure luck, the generosity of the UUA, and constant heart-rending cries for support, like if they died the very life blood of the liberal Church would dry up forever. Mention Harvard or Meadville and you get a look of piteous condescension, of puzzled hurt. Starr King lives on a shoestring and a prayer (or meditation), except for their department of public relations and printing expenditures. I don't mind that. It lends flair to their self-image of persecution and creativity.

It's in more important matters that they need help. The catalog quotes (white ink on green paper)—after all it's spring—a poem of Cummings about how you and I may not hurry spring with a thousand poems, but nobody will stop it With All The Policemen In The World. Deification of flower power into an irresistible and omnipotent Cosmic Force is typical of Starr King theologizing.

It's at this point that I send on to them a recent quote from Wallace Robbins, our minister in Worcester, a quote they might consider printing in their next catalog (red ink on brown maybe). By the way, Dr. Robbins is a former president of Meadville.

"Nature is not a goddess, but a creature like ourselves, she can be deformed, weakened and killed as can a man ... let us know that to greet the spring with joy is not enough, we must greet the spring ethically, training ourselves to withhold our engineered strength, which if unrestrained will overwhelm wetlands and hills, running brooks and quiet leaf-mold. We must greet this spring with determination to defend our birthright, to protect our ancient vitalities and to align ourselves on the side of total life."

May your next catalog be more ecological, O Starr King, and your theology more biodegradable.

THE BEST MINISTERS
I KNOW

I ask myself what men in our denomination do I admire most? I write down ten names.

Then I ask what these ten have in common, why I like them. They range in age from their 30's to late 60's. I've known them from 6 years to 20 years. (It takes time for cream to rise.) Here is what I discover.

1—All of them have enormous egos, but most know it and pray about it and every day try again to shape up and fly right.

2—All are married, fathers, and masculine; big, fine voices, strong and athletic of body, but free to express their feminine component and maternal impulses.

3—All are great talkers but, with the exception of 2, can greatly enjoy hearing other great talkers. All have wide-ranging enthusiasms, intellectual depth and some scholarly interests and pursuits.

4—All are sinners. I mean, to my surprise, that all of them have been wrong on some important denominational issues over the years. None is afraid to be in the wrong with two or three. Most are slightly narcissistic and compulsively energetic.

5—All are saints in their love of life and dedicated to making it more humane. 7 of them even know how to go about doing it.

6—Seven of ten will answer your letters; 4 of them will give indication in their reply of having read yours.

7—All are outstanding preachers, that is they speak with conviction, literacy, power.

8—All have balanced ministries; personal-social, science-art, tradition-novelty, pastor-prophet.

9—None is guilty of the following: sentimentality—though each can pour on the sentiment; manipulation, though none is ashamed to use his powers of persuasion; sanctimoniousness, though each is deeply religious; betrayal of confidence, though each knows more than any gossip in town; bitterness, though each is capable of wrath; and colored socks, though each acknowledges the right of others to wear them.

10—All are sharply defined, idiosyncratic, individual, unique. They have presence. They stand out. While co-operative, gregarious, social to a fault, they don't blend in. As a matter of fact, if you put one in a blender he'd break the blades, crack the glass and bounce around like a steel fork. I hope you are always fortunate enough to have ministers like them, and help to keep them that way.

MY PLATFORM

It's not too early to announce my UUA platform: Fiscal responsibility and bold new programming. I will:

1—Demand the Channing Memorial Church in Newport, R.I. give up possession of Channing's pulpit robe and return it to the UUA, cleaned, pressed, and with new arm shields.

2—Kill what's left of the Interdistrict plan and establish a system of State Conventions.

3—Keep in better touch with our centers in Saginaw, Altoona, Walla Walla, Jonesboro, West Paris, Uxbridge, and Excelsior, Minnesota.

4—Reduce UUA salaries by 25%. Savings from this thrift to go to augment cost-of-living adjustment for new executive committee.

5—Abolish two term limit and retirement rules. Keep Joe Barth and Ed Darling forever to greet at front door of 25 Beacon, in green knickers and yellow vests, to hand out balloons, and beat up each year the entering new ministers as part of their orientation.

6—Affirm, in an age of rootlessness and anxiety, stability, continuity, tradition. Carry over men like Hopkins, Benson, Raible, in shipping department. For pilgrims to Boston: ex-leaders Greeley and West will be exhumed and displayed under glass in lobby, perhaps on rotating basis.

7—Switch Virginia Mulley to head Department of Ministry. I don't know a minister who wouldn't be thrilled to have her handle his file. Dr. Spencer will plan our General Assemblies, with orders to hold them from now on in the Bahamas, during February. We need to emphasize the international thrust of our outreach.

8—Hire competent women in knee boots in every department and office, in dominant positions.

9—Combat male sexist pigism. I will appoint a blue ribbon panel of 35 ministers to investigate. To get the "little woman's" view I'll appoint a female to this commission. She can be secretary.

10—Solve financial worries. Kick LRY out of building for bad conduct, gratitude and smell. Turn 6th floor over to bar, casino, massage parlor. Fund raising dept. can be redeployed as croupiers, masseuses. Board room will have private elevator to 6th floor.

11—Stay in Boston. No more ego-tripping over the continent on your hard-earned money. (With that 6th floor, who needs to travel?)

12—Bring us together. Sundays I'll greet before service at Arlington St., leave in time to be seen kneeling at King's Chapel, slip out to Community Church to challenge the speaker, slide out for after-Church clam juice at prophetic First Church, and dash over to Charles St. Meeting House in time to knead clay and carry a sign. Sunday afternoons I'll edit the book begun by my predecessors, *Integrity on the Run.*

You can put planks in this platform by sending cash (no checks or money orders) in a plain brown envelope to yours truly. Our good will is your receipt.

110

CHRISTMAS
AND LIBERALS

Liberals like Christmas. It is our favorite religious holiday. It's all about birth, creation, light and hope. We believe in these words—birth, creation, light, hope—and we have for centuries.

All religious groups have their special emphasis—their views on what is most worthwhile to observe and celebrate. In other traditions some holidays get more thought and ritual attention. With us it is Christmas. We don't emphasize Lent, Good Friday, speaking in tongues at Pentecost, or the marble-jawed tombs opening up their sleepers at Easter. That's all a little too much.

With Christmas, it's different. Here we are at home. We share in the deeps this holy time. And with the help of a little egg-nog we sing as lustily as our neighbors about angels and shepherds and wise men and virgins running all over the place.

If we happen to be politically liberal, as well as theologically liberal, we have a field day at Christmas time. Christmas is built for us!

Fair-housing advocates make hay with the dramatic illustration of the turn-down at the inn; for those pushing for community health and slum clearance, what a tale we can pull out of the manger! (A manger is a trough for feeding animals. It's from the same root as "mangy," meaning squalid, infested with disease of parasites in pigs and cows.)

For those working on the racial front or the United Nations, there are the three wise men—one of whom is obviously an Oriental, and another, Balthalzar, a precursor of Eldridge Cleaver.

For us pacifists and anti-war types, the Christmas story has better slogans than Norman Cousins, the Nation, Progressive, and the Christian Century combined.

We mail each year to friends (who live in the suburbs and believe the same things we do) Christmas cards with mini-sermons and pleas for peace. We write touching things like, "Why can't we have Christmas the whole year around?" or "Why can't the world be decent to each other, like we are in our neighborhood?" or "The only way we can live with ourselves is to work harder and harder and harder for peace NOW!"

At Christmas time we liberals love to point out the contradiction of celebrating Christmas in the midst of warfare. We feel moral disdain for the general populace who don't understand the exquisite pain this contradiction causes in our liberal sensibility. (All those "ignorant armies" clashing by night for which we of course are not responsible, having previously eschewed both ignorance and hostility in our own neighborhoods.)

We like Christmas, too, because Jesus is a baby and there is not yet any anger; no judgment, no paradox, no decision, no pain, no betrayal. True, Mary ponders some things in her heart, but it is probably whether to send the child to Oberlin, Swarthmore or Antioch. The good guys win in the Christmas story, in spite of Herod and the inn-keeper, and liberals like that. It fits our metaphysics.

111

I am a Uni-Uni, a liberal, and I plan to enjoy my Christmas very much. But I think we should remind ourselves that it is not the only holy day in Christendom, lest our rightful emphasis become a lop-sided, foolish idol. The realities we joyfully sing at Christmas time—growth, love, hope, creation, triumph, new birth—have their opposites in decay, hate, despair, wreckage, defeat and death.

We liberals need, in paraphrase of Marvell, to recall other seasons at our backs —lents, good Fridays, and Easters, hurrying near. Only so can faith be whole. Merry Christmas to all, and prayers for our time of need.

CENSORSHIP OF THE PENTAGON PAPERS

Our Beacon Press, believing with Channing that the issue of war stands above all others in need of "solemn inquisition," put it on the line Oct. 22 in publishing the 4-volume set *The Senator Gravel Edition of the Pentagon Papers*. It is on Vietnam. Our government hoped to keep it secret from us.

What motive for trying to stop the printing of these papers? Honorable of course. As honorable as the Long Parliament's with whom John Milton pleaded in 1643. The government, then as now, simply wanted an "Order for the Regulating of Printing, and for suppressing ... Seditious ... and unlicensed Pamphlets, to the great defamation of ... Government." Milton, a free Churchman, didn't buy that line.

"Give me," he answered, "the liberty to know, to utter, and to argue freely according to conscience, above all liberties."

So our small Press (in contrast to 6 large commercial and university publishing houses) risked $100,000 to back up the forefathers' pledge of a national policy for public discussion of public questions. That's what the 1st amendment—that government shall make no law abridging the freedom of the press—is all about.

But men like Johnson and Nixon forget. The Pentagon visited our Headquarters and the FBI looked over our bank records. They tried to make us scare and conform to their Long Parliament wishes. They tried to do what a bully always tried to do to his would-be victim: make him timid and obliging, through threat and harrassment.

I used to avoid a bully by taking another route home. That's good strategy. But it won't work if the bully stands at your front door. For this reason we need the concerted indignation of our Church people across the continent. It is unwise but understandable to neglect to care for freedom when its issues are at another's door. But it is a yellow streak and mortal blindness to allow the marauder to enter at the hearth of your own faith.

We stop government bullying at our own doorsteps or nowhere. The next visit of the FBI is not at 25 Beacon Street in Boston, Mass., but at the address of your local Church. It's but a step there to the home of your minister and your local Church treasurer. And finally your own. When that happens you can get ready to have your face opened with a pistol butt and watch a whole library burn on the rug of your living room floor.

Secrecy and censorship are the first weapons in the hands of tyrants: give them these and they will take the rest. But if the free press succumbs it will not be at the hands of a clumsy federal police force. It will be because the owners of Beacon Press, you and I, through laziness, fear, disregard, turn it over without charge or murmur to those monsters of unfaith masked in the honorable guise of national security. John Milton didn't buy their line. Don't you.

You can whack the bully by buying the books. In the $20 or $45 set. (Beacon Press, 25 Beacon, Boston 02108, or phone 742-2100.) I don't care if you read them. Give them to your libraries, schools, (mine went to Weymouth's Tufts last week) or post them in your home, your office window, as symbols for your neighbors and the world to see. The issue is not your opinion on Vietnam but on the right of free men to know.

My friends and fellow Churchmen, a bully has crossed a sacred threshold. As a tigress smites for her cubs, so may you protect your own Press. The 4-volumn set—place it with ceremony in your home, in every Church, library, fellowship lounge.

Some small cost to knock the bully off the steps. Some small cost to hail old freedom's martyrs, to say thanks for the forefathers' gift. Some small cost for peace in days after.

Advance, free Church, Advance.

ON BEING RECENTLY CIRCUMCISED

In making hospital calls ministers are called upon to hear agonized confessions, to pray with the wasted and dying, to be close to the elements of breath and blood and joy and pain, to wait with, listen to, talk with human souls in the depths of life. It is a great privilege, one interrupted only occasionally by a strange perversity of association.

In any ailment concerning the genitals of the patient the relationship of honesty and human meeting is disrupted. Instead of being a minister one must learn, like a graduate of the Fletcher School of Diplomacy, to speak in the scented prose of verbal anesthetic and double-talk. Brain tumors, bad lungs, ruptured spleens, broken bones, fine, but when it comes to the central crotch of humankind, No, an anatomical taboo slams the door of dialogue. Your bedded parishioner and you must chat away like cupie dolls viewing a slide show on Hawaii.

How silly. The intestinal tract, though very close by, is not under the taboo. "Excruciating rectal itch" is in the public domain. Our "irregularity," how we vomit, and what, all this is O.K. But not matters to do with penises and vaginas. I decided long ago I'd not contribute to this conspiracy of silent denegration of sexuality.

So let me tell you about my operation. Last week I took the 7 a.m. bus to Beth Israel hospital to be circumcised. A wart on the foreskin had to go, though one of the 3 interns who witnessed the operation asked the surgeon, Dr. Sears, how he could grow one just like it. The operating room was in an uproar for an hour. I was at my wittiest (subconscious fear is the source of much of our best humor) and the 3 interns and one nurse (male, alas) were at their best in bawdy repartee.

The operation was televised in the U.S. and telestared throughout Europe, we averred, with eastern Europe blacked out. We saw no reason to let the Commies in on this. To compensate for the absence of a female intern, which we all lamented, one of the doctors held my hand and told me I was cute. A high point of hilarity was reached when the surgeon said oops, sorry, back to the drawing boards. It took me a minute to catch on to the humor of that one.

I was sore for a week, but feel good about shedding my Philistine past. If any of you gentlemen in the parish have been circumcised recently, drop in for coffee; it would be fun to compare notes; it's not everyone you can talk with in detail about your operation.

To anyone who might be offended by the above ("an unpardonable breach of good taste," "a gaffe of incredible vulgarity")—before you cancel your pledge or write the Prudential Committee, remember that the King James Bible mentions foreskins 12 times and circumcision 87 times. And that's real literchur.

Selah. I have done my duty, my small part in cutting through the genital taboo. And rest easy, any of you displeased. I will not have the occasion to mention my foreskin again.

115

OBSCENITY

With changing standards many people are having trouble defining obscenity. Some are confused and wondering if anything is obscene anymore. My answer is Yes, obscenity does exist. It is real and rampant. Let me define it for you, in a dozen ways.

Obscenity is:

1. Mugging an old person.
2. The mind of the censor.
3. Shooting animals for fun.
4. Gossiping to hurt a good name.
5. "Nigger" on the lips of a racist.
6. Smashing glass on the beach and leaving it there.
7. TV ads clamoring to deodorize all God's creation.
8. Rich doctors opposing national health care for the poor.
9. A gas chamber at Buckenwald (or electric chair at Walpole).
10. A rayon bow stuck in the middle of a bouquet of fresh flowers.
11. Demanding release of our pilots so they can rip open more children with their bombs.
12. Cutting down redwoods, poisoning rivers, and putting industrialists on pollution control boards.

That's what obscenity is.

GENERATION GAP

One twelfth of Vietnam is defoliated. As the Nazis used Spain in the 1930's to test out new weaponry, so we use Vietnam to test out and experiment with crop-killing, plant-destroying poisons, over an area as large as our state of Massachusetts.

What disastrous consequences occur is evidently of no matter to our government. After all, Vietnam is a long way away, we are dealing with Asians, and we are serving the cause of democracy, like the inquisitor in the middle ages who burned heretics in order to save their souls.

What has happened to the conscience of the nation? Does it reside only in the young? And are we forcing that conscience to express itself only by violent means? I am sorry that Humphrey was not allowed to give his speech at the University of Massachusetts, but he has been awhoring with men like Thieu and Maddox and brutal Chicago police; what does he expect? I am sorry that a mob burned down a Bank in Santa Barbara, but when avaricious wealth persists unpunished in its despoliation of the coastal water, what else should it expect?

A law of reciprocity is at work in history; violence breeds counter violence. When this nation begins to deal seriously with its massive sins of imperialism, racism, exploitation, economic injustice, and dehumanization, it will find the conscience of youth again eager and co-operative. What they see at present is the Establishment's double talk and big lies. (I have seen an official government report which makes the claim that our defoliation program in Vietnam is good for the soil.)

Thank God for the generation gap, the student revolt, the refusal to sit in silence amidst this madness in our national life.

CHEERS TO
GEORGE KAPLAN

In a Nov. 17, 1860 Journal entry, Thoreau tells us how they did things in West Acton. He was walking along the Harvard turnpike when he saw a rock larger than a man could lift lying in the road. He puzzled about how it got there and about the fact that it was a peculiar black.

On his return journey at twilight near the same spot he saw a man running off for cover behind a hill as fast as he could go. Thoreau thought for a moment and then it occurred to him to run the other way as fast as he could go. And just in time. When he had dashed a few rods off went two blasts, hurtling rocks through the air. Fortunately none hit him. Now Thoreau understood that the big stone had been blackened by powder. He concludes the account laconically: "They looked out for themselves, but for nobody else. This is the way they do things in West Acton."

I am sure that none of the good people of West Acton today would be as thoughtless as their townsman of yesteryear. Yet the reminder is there for all of us about blasting off before thinking of consequences and without concern for others.

This season my annual West Acton Turnpike Award for Thoughtfulness goes to George Kaplan, couturier in fur, of 730 Fifth Avenue, New York. Recently he pledged, because of deep trouble in the ecological balance of the animal world, to refuse to buy or sell any more furs of rare animals whose species are endangered. As a furrier he proposes to make it unfashionable to wear the skins of leopards, tigers, the cheetah, polar bear, Spanish lynx, jaguar, red wolf, sea otter, ocelot and vicuna. Even though it would be more immediately profitable to look out only for himself.

The world could use more people like that, in places like Paris, Saigon, Hanoi, Moscow, Washington and several other towns along the pike.

I SEND THESE GIFTS

Christmas gifts: I send a holy salute through prison walls to Phil and Dan Berrigan and Cesar Chavez; Tillich's Systematic Theology to Billy Graham to help him in his initial exploration of the Christian faith; Hathaway shirts to King Hussein from Moshe Dyan; a box of Dutch chocolates to Paul VI from all his pals in Holland; to Nixon an old plowshare cleverly retooled into a bayonet to help him in his quest for peace; to Khrushchev for his memoirs, his courageous trip to Iowa and his tears at Kennedy's death, our guest room for him and the Mrs., corn on the cob and Bailey's Pleasant Street Vodka anytime.

A medal to the first Church bureaucrat who doesn't blame all his problems on lack of funds; a powder puff to the UUA statistician for the clouds and cushions around our recent losses in churches, R.E., membership and income; three-and-a-half bushels of self-confidence and the money for a good shrink to all ministers recently fired from their jobs; and to our honey-mooning Interdistrict Rep, a map showing roads to Church groups within the Interdistrict.

To other institutions beyond the Church: New England Telephone, a buzz, a silence, a crazy whine; Boston Edison, an hour's hover in a helicopter over your stinking smoke stacks; to passenger railroad executives, a cross tie in your Lincoln manifold and a steel rail in your power steering; to the chain of command at Mylai, God's mercy, none of mine.

Christmas cards to all our old girl friends to remind them how unlucky they are for not having taken us when they had the chance; exit visas from the land of capitalist cliches ("Why don't you lazy bums show more initiative?") to all the high-salaried execs out of jobs for the first time, and a free enterprize opportunity to join in the left wing of the Democratic party; speaking of the highly paid, a purgative in the dinosaur stomach of the American Medical Association to remind them we are more concerned with our health than in their profits and propaganda; and to my hero of the hour, 43-year-old footballer George Blanda, from all his middle-age admirers, the title deed to all land in Florida sought by Ponce de Leon.

Finally to life, a grudging hello for new chances, in spite of the outrage and disaster entailed.

ANGELA DAVIS, NOT GUILTY

While I rejoice in the acquittal of Angela Davis, I am not fooled.

Why? Because her accusers knew she was innocent before they tried her. They used the trial itself as a means of intimidation and punishment, a common technique in these repressive Nixon years.

Angela was locked in a steel cage for 16 months. Her accusers moved free, with sun and rain on their faces, moonlight, blossoms, love. Angela was confined to a cell to eat bitter bread and wonder if California would gas her to death. This was her punishment for being a brilliant black and a communist.

So do not let the moment of rejoicing deceive. Justice has not been done. Should a victim of rape be expected to thank her assaulters?

The law of our forefathers was intended as a shield to protect dissenters like Angela; not intended as a weapon to wipe them out. So do not rejoice. Hear instead the rattle of irons. Ominous and wicked forces are loose in American life. They would have us wake up in chains.

THE BATTLE OF BRITAIN

Few there are who receive the recognition they deserve during their own lifetime. We take for granted in this unjust world of ours the posthumous character of most of the praise we give. What happened to Jesus is a parable for most every man. So much that is great goes unsung and Easters arrive too late.

A latter day instance of this sad truth is the recent death (February 15) of the greatest unsung hero of World War II, a certain Hugh Caswall T. Dowding.

It was he who deserves credit for the development of the Spitfire and Hurricane fighters; it was he who prevented what would have been their disastrous use in the losing battle of France; it was he who built the early warning radar posts to signal from the coast the approach of enemy planes; it was he who directed the battle that decisive summer and fall of 1940 when all that was decent and humane in western culture was under the most dire threat from the Nazi hordes.

To accomplish what he did he had to oppose cherished doctrines, accepted beliefs, bureaucratic powers, and vain and foolish men. Within a month after the Battle of Britain he was dismissed and within two years retired to his home in Tunbridge Wells in Kent where, until the recent publication of a book and movie, he lived unwept, unhonored, and unsung.

His latter days were spent secluded and in the investigation of the occult nonsense of spirtualism. He came to believe he had physical contact with the young men who had died under his command. How pitiful and how terribly sweet.

And now in this unjust world of ours the posthumous praise begins. That is the way life is. But he had a son, an only son, who succeeds him. His name is Derek Hugh T. Dowding and he is a Wing Commander in the Royal Air Force.

KIDNEY MACHINES

The refusal of our government to make available dialysis machines—artificial kidneys—is responsible for the deaths of thousands of Americans every year. I don't know how your logic runs, but mine tells me this is tantamount to premeditated mass murder.

If a baby were struggling face down under water at the seashore and you were there to lift him into the air for breath, and you refused, you would be a monster, an incarnation of the dread enemy of human kind. And if you said you would help on condition that the parents turn over $40,000, you would still be a monster, a calculating monster.

So with our nation. If we were helpless, poor, unable to assist, then there is no crime. Only sorrow. But when the powerful, rich and able turn their backs, walk away from a simple and humane task, then, then my friends, we commit crime.

No problem for the rich. The economic barriers to uremic disease therapy are easily circumvented. Or, I'm sure, if you are a president or senator. Or one of the lucky ones chosen (10%) by a "Life and Death Committee" who play God (albeit anonymously and without pay) and decide who shall be treated and who shall die.

Our nation's indifference to this easily solvable problem says something, I'm afraid, quite sickening about the condition of our national spirit. Condemning thousands of our fellow citizens to certain death by poisoning—slow and painful, who have committed no crime—is an act of such monstrous criminality that it could be done only by automatons and zombies.

DOWN WITH
MOTHER'S DAY

Mother's Day should be abolished. It is a sentimental contrivance of florists, candy-makers, the Pentagon, the ecologically illiterate and male chauvinist pigs who enjoy tossing occasional bones to bedraggled housewives.

The holiday has no tradition or wide appeal. It is without connection to ancient and lusty rituals, it is ignored the world over, and its vintage here in America is recent and raw—Philadelphia, Pa., 1907.

Why a day for motherhood? Is it not but one of many roles a woman might be born to? Why not an Aunt's Day, a Niece's Day, Single Women's Day, Married Women's Day? Why should procreation win the prize on this population-packed globe? Nothing wrong with babies, up to two, but no special virtue either.

Women have babies for many reasons, not all meritorious: because they are taught they ought, because they like to play with dolls, need company, because of tedium, or accident, to get ahead of the Joneses, to have someone little to push around for twenty years. Why a medal for this?

In place of a day for mothers, (I'm no simple iconoclast), how about honoring the people who adopt orphans? With extra flowers for bringing home for love and rearing the half-breeds, the undesirable, the injured, the incomplete. Now that would be a day to celebrate!

Father's Day? A mere afterthought of the Tie Industry and Bell Telephone, I leave it out of our discussion.

But many women most important in our lives never conceive or carry. You have your own precious list, I'm sure. I think of Emily Dickinson, Florence Nightingale, Miss Steckelberg, a teacher of mine—I forget the course matter but never her generosity; I think of an RE director in Oklahoma, many more. These "barren" ladies I'll vote to kneel in honor to any day, in spring, winter, summer or fall, for their surpassing, supra-uterine gifts to creation. May their fruitful tribe multiply over the earth!

We are indebted to mothers for half a life and many of us (myself included) for much more. But the much more hasn't to do with motherhood. It has to do with caring, respect, knowledge, responsibility. These qualities attach to persons, not ovaries.

So down with this cult of womb worship, this beatification of breeding, this Fallopian foolery. Personhood, not impregnation, is the chief end of woman as of man. Mother's Day is an idol and it's time to tie her tubes.

If Anna Jarvis can proclaim Mother's Day from a Methodist Church in Philadelphia in 1907, I can proclaim Woman's Day from a Universalist Church in South Weymouth, Mass. in 1971. Happy Woman's Day, ladies!

THE GROSS,
YES, THE GROSS
NATIONAL PRODUCT

The best news story of 1971 is on page 61 of the January 4 *Times:*
OKLAHOMA CITY (UPI)—Harold Arnold, a watchman, deposited 35 cents in a City Hall vending machine and reached in to get a sandwich. When the machine caught his hand, he pulled out his pistol and shot the machine twice. The second shot severed some wires and he got his hand out.

It reminds me of the third chapter of Ezekiel: "Son of man, I have made you a watchman for the house of Israel; when you hear a word from my mouth, you shall give them warning from me."

I favor strict gun control, even for watchmen. I am also a 90 per cent pacifist. But I confess that Mr. Arnold has become overnight a hero of mine, a brilliant comet in a dark sky.

I wish he could have been in Washington, D.C. to see the unveiling of the new GNP Clock at the Commercial Building. This brightly lit machine tells us the value of all the goods made and all the services done for us—the gross national product—in the past year.

Our President was there for ceremonies because this giant cash register went over one trillion dollars for the first time. "We hope to keep it moving and perhaps move it faster in the years ahead," said Mr. Nixon.

We are supposed to look at the GNP Clock, going up $2,000 a second, and say how wonderful it is to grow. That is where I want Mr. Arnold to come in.

The Clock doesn't tell us about the purpose of the growth, the reasons for the production, the significance of the services, the priorities of our spending, the moral worth of our wealth, or the stench of our wickedness.

It tells of luxury, not of malnutrition. It tells of expansion for faster airplanes, not of decline in mass transport. It registers the value of new cars but not the pollution they cause. It says little about ecological crime, supported on a grand scale by the largest consumer of natural resources in world history. It fails to mention that a three-billion-dollar-a-year garbage bill is part of our growth.

It fails to mention other goods and services that belong to our growth: the cost of plastic body bags, embalming fluid, aluminum coffins, air-freight and burial grounds for our dead soldiers; the cost of soap flake and tooth brush advertisements, the booze for six million alcoholics; the pay for guardsmen who shot students in Jackson, Mississippi and Kent, Ohio; the food and cages for 200,000 men in our prisons, the services to put up Out-of-Order signs on utilities across our nation.

What Mr. Nixon didn't tell us about our first trillion GNP (apart from its inflationary stuffing) is that no sane man would brag about a volume of goods and services that includes 6 lbs. of plant killing chemicals for every man, woman and child in Vietnam. This is not of our wealth, but of our depravity.

Much of our growth is disorganized, chaotic, unregulated and destructive. The growth Mr. Nixon praises is the philosophy of the cancer cell—wild, unconfined growth for growth's sake. The GNP Clock is a monster of callousness and trickery. The purpose of a GNP is to serve man, not destroy him. As Isaiah put it, (1,22) "Your silver has become dross."

Bring in Harold Arnold.

GOD SAVE THE QUEEN

A word about why I am an Anglophile if not an Anglican. Compared with our British brethren we are a nation of cowered commuting sheep. Consider, for example, the contrasting response of our two nations to contrived trouble and sabotaged service on passenger trains. In America the public has submitted itself so meekly for so long that it has practically no rail service left; commuters who would prefer a crack train into, say Boston, must crawl instead by auto or bus through monoxide fogs in constant danger of being up-ended, side-swiped, or otherwise insulted.

The techniques designed by rail management to drive away customers, in order to provide final excuse for discontinuation of all service, have worked— surley conductors, filthy floors, unconscionable delays, discarding of sleepers, jettisoning of lounges, diners, bars, coffee counters, even temperature controls. Until today it is no longer a question of diners. We don't even have trains.

Contrast this to our British cousins (who, by the way, easily could have burned down the entire nation in 1812, not just the White House, if they had opted to feel genuinely irritated; and who could have beaten the colonies into an imperial pulp in 1776 had they felt actually put upon in a keen way).

Picture a morning commuter train an hour out of London; management, British Railways, tries to slip one over on the passengers; kippers, those spiced and smoked sea trout, are quietly removed from the menu, along with a choice of scrambled over fried eggs and brown bread toast over white. It also decides to charge for the side of tomatoes with bacon and eggs, whether ordered or not. The excuse seems reasonable enough by most of the standards of the outside world. The Brighton Belle's run, from 9:25 to 10:25 into London, is indeed short, and the larger menu inconveniences the railway in short-order speed and economic return.

The English commuter, however, does not gather his standards from lesser breeds outside the realm. He peruses the new menu, pronounces it shocking, and then, commoner and peer alike, rises like Mars in the scepter'd isle, this other Eden, demi-paradise, in righteous wrath rolling from Runnymede on down to the present day, to demand, petition, and protest for a return to a better way. And there is no question who will win the battle. British Railways doesn't have a chance. Each of its customers is a one-man Ralph Nader. Englishmen do not cower.

In such larger tasks as saving Christian civilization from a protracted Dark Age of Nazi enslavement or in simply preserving the subtler dignities of commuter travel and the amenities of a dining-car breakfast, we can count on Englishmen. Where similar menu incidents were perpetrated in our own country the hapless commuter was bludgeoned into immediate acquiescence. Today you can't buy coffee in leaky paper cups.

That is why I am an Anglophile. And may God save the Queen.

126

SUBWAY RIDING

Subways are bad. I don't know any place that can drain off your humanity faster. After Ashmont it gets more and more crowded. Packed in like smoked oysters; no space for individuality, no room for freedom. So everybody makes a point of not looking at everybody else, and everybody else makes a point of not looking back. Hard, blank stares to nowhere. I suppose if you smile you get socked in the nose, or have a pervert crawl all over you. It is easier to trust when there is room to negotiate.

Three more stops, no body gets off, more jam on. My enemy Sartre takes on truth: no exit, hell is other people. It is eight in the morning. Passengers are grim. What will we look like at five tonight?

Hold on to the pole: six other hands on it, some hairy, none alike, none touching, except during lurches of the car. Many attractive people, bright clothes. But nobody is happy. The hippy type students look as morose as the tailored bourgeoisie. I want to break through this sullen anonymity. What a place to evangelize, to preach! On second thought I wouldn't open my mouth for a million bucks. On third thought people might like it, the chance to look, hear, relate. It might mean—communication between people, rather than this November cemetery of gaunt, accusing, lifeless stones. I'll preach on "The Fallacies of Existentialism."

I suspect we don't like to turn to stones. It is a necessity here to protect one's soul, one's privacy and integrity of inner life, to hold off the outward physical intrustions of uninvited humanity. I bet we all wish we could put on a button saying "Pardon me. I have been forced by a wicked monster to turn temporarily into stone. It is not permanent. I don't like being this way. Watch me turn back into a human being at Park Street Station."

More passengers push on. I am next to an obese lady with a glass eye. I am resigned to this. It is all right. All my life it has been this way, on busses, trains, airplanes, now the subway. So my surprise is doubly great when a gorgeous young black is forced to lodge tightly next to my body. Afro hairdo, an inch from my face. What hair. I smell Tabu. I look at her long, lovely chocolate neck. Shall I tell her I am a friendly vampire? With the forefinger of my free hand I rub my front teeth—tell them to stay where they are and mind their own business. Think of the headlines: "Minister chomps, etc. ..." I'm in enough trouble. I don't need that. Who would come to my aid? BAC, BAWA, ACLU, my wife? At least they can't accuse me of prejudice.

Finally, Park Street: fresh air, room, trees! Hey, people, look! Don't worry about the weirdos! We're here; the sun is shining! Fellow stones, please turn back to humans! Smile, for God's sake, smile someone!

FLICKAHOLIA

Muslim mystics never talk about their relationship to God. I have never talked about my relationship to movies. Until now.

I am a flickaholic. I've been known to take in 13 movies a week. Usually I can control myself. Sometimes I go for months without taking a single flick, but the temptation's always there, and if I take a single look, it's too late: before breakfast I head for the marquees on Tremont Street, dash across the Common for another before noon, then have one for the road by the subway, then home to urge my wife to join me for an evening of double features at the Cameo. (The Cameo plays 80 yards from the back porch of the parsonage—like putting a bee next to a molasses barrel.)

I start out seeing the best movies. I try to remain discriminating, keep sober. I mail off memos to the Globe movie critics, pointing out their errors, which they never acknowledge; I see more movies, eyes bloodshot now, my money running out, I hit the X-rated flicks, stagger away and finally bottom out watching pitiful horror movies on late night TV in my own living room—the ultimate degradation. I promise Cora I'll never do it again. She forgives, fixes coffee.

Hoping to turn my shame to some redemptive use, I decided this week to confess all and to commend to you a few of the better movies from my last bender, excluding The Seduction Of Inga during which I blacked out, and The Ten Commandments during which I vomited.

Do see, in moderation: The French Connection, Sometimes A Great Notion, Cabaret, The Hospital, Diamonds Are Forever, Straw Dogs, Klute, The Clockwork Orange, The Godfather, Polanski's Macbeth, The Trojan Women.

I haven't had a movie in several weeks now. I notice "The Last Picture Show" at Abbey Cinema II starts at 1:30 today. I have a friend in Dedham, a fellow minister and flickaholic. Maybe I better call him. It's not good to be alone. I thought I might—I have to go to Boston to see my docotr anyway—I thought I might drop by for a quick looksee, and, "The Garden of the Finzi-Continis" is at the Exeter and, well, just one or two won't do any harm ... I can handle my flicks.

MY LAST NIGHT
AT THE OPERA

I saw La Traviata last week, my last grand opera. It is difficult to describe how pitiful it is. La Triviata all the way. Not the music—Verdi is irresistibly lovely; not the singing—no engineering yet in brass or gut can match God's fashioning of our human voice. It is grand opera as such. Opera is a mistake.

In his essay on Dryden Eliot remarks that the 19th century had, like every other, limited tastes and peculiar fashions and was unaware of its own limitations. Verdi lived from 1813 to 1901.

I ventured to the opera because I was given a $15 ticket by a man of culture (l'homme de culture) who had a previous engagement. I note the night of the opera the Bruins beat St. Louis 5-3.

First the setting: Hynes Auditorium, the War Memorial, a theatre of tasteless and brutal strenght, fit for Nazi pageants and aerial strategems. It is designed to exhibit bulldozers, Imperials, anti-air-craft guns, oil derricks, battle cruisers and other accoutrements of our civilization. It is a blasted heath congealed in chrome, plastics and gargantuan vacancies. La Traviata fit in perfectly. I figured it would take my longest pass, 60 yards, to throw a football into the balconies on either side, and even with my $15 seat, another long bomb to hit the consumptive soprano in the stomach at stage center.

Three intermissions totalled 1 hour and 22 minutes. It takes grandiose time to move grandiose scenery. Between acts opera lovers sip sicky-sweet champagne— a dollar for 2½ oz. The house clears $10 a bottle after taxes, wages and lawsuits.

To the opera itself—the final concentration of cornball melodrama and escapist sentimentality, all taken seriously. I watched educated people fawn from 8 to 11:30 before the most egregious implausibilities and applaud between acts the narcissistic perpetrators of same. The audience, moneyed and tuxedoed, is the same at heart as the one who watches the wrestlers of grunt and groan.

Like the businessman in Church who leaves his brain at the office, it's all feeling and furore. At worst it is the inauthentic at home with the incredible. It is an art form that unhinges rather than hones our humanity. See *Nietzsche Contra Wagner*.

The last act of La Traviata consists of the heroine singing herself to death, collapsing over one side of the bed, then the other, alternating this weird gymnastic with sobbing recitatives on life's brevity and complaints about medicare. The stage is bathed in ghoulish green. Violins sob. Alfredo arrives, with a song in his heart. She collapses. He sings. She recovers. Sings to him. Collapses again. Is revived. Alfredo works her over—weeps on her breasts, groans in her groin, paws at her body, shouts in her ears, spatters her face with spit. The treatment fails. Alfredo's not a doctor but a greenhorn necrophiliac. Violetta, seasoned courteasan though she is, has taken all she can take, and dies.

Some traditions, conventions should be dropped, turned off; like bombing civilian populations, or kneeling to royalty. Opera is such a convention. It demands a suspension of disbelief no serious person can grant—unless anesthetized by booze and heady pretensions to Kulcher. As a parody taking itself seriously opera is also demeaning to music and song and drama. It's bad art.

But let me close on a hopeful note. Grand opera, I have been informed, faces a grave financial crisis. Its supporters say it may not survive.

Let us pray.

ERROL FLYNN AND CO.

The first heroes, mythic figures, to surface to remembrance from my summons, until I was almost 12 in 1941 and we all fell out of grace, my first heroes looming larger than our lakes beyond Green Bay, Ann Arbor or Detroit, brood still: Don Hutson, his name intagliod on my shoulder pads—I swore it was his personal autograph and that I'd catch footballs forever. Hank Greenberg, over the radio the crack of his bat (58 homers in '38) still sharp 150 miles away from my town, leader of a distant pantheon of Tigers. I revered. And Tom Harmon, breaking, twisting, galloping thru, oh, my head was full of trumpets and what pride in Michigan earth!

Not all was sports: I pasted a scrapbook on Gene Autry, another on Errol Flynn. How I worshipped him—Robin Hood, Gentleman Jim Corbett, Capt. Courtney of the Royal Flying Corps. When blood trickled at the corner of his mouth and he went down in Dawn Patrol (the first movie where my hero died) I was disconsolate for weeks, maybe years. With a child's prescience, from that moment when a Von Richter pilot swooped with his fatal rat-tat-tat thru my ace's plane, with me sitting helpless, grounded, in the rococo splendor of the State Theatre in Kalamazoo, from that moment I was anti-German for life. Neitzsche and Lotte Lenya are the only exceptions. To this day I carry a fantasy that all Volkswagen owners will trade in their wretched little Wagnerian burps for cleanly green MG's.

During his real life trial I followed Flynn every day in the Chicago Tribune. With heart beating against my ribs, I'd sneak from article to the huge Webster to look up the strange and overwhelming words—carnal, statutory, illicit, intimate relations. I couldn't figure out the last except that Flynn said it wasn't so and I believed him with all my strength until the jury set him free. I wrote him immediately out of the corny depths of my soul, "Thank God for American justice." He sent me another picture of himself. Jesus I loved him.

Speaking of Jesus, he never took. The pinkish gown, the silly cane, being nice to girls and sheep, what a yawn. Samson though revisits. In Vacation Bible School a teacher made a magic struggle on a felt board with cut-out brightly colored figures leaping on and off. I remember Samson beating hell out of a lion and I liked that a lot.

I had some anonymous heroes—the French horn players in the Nutcracker Suite. Geo. Washington's spirit never grasped me. Lincoln's did. He was 6-ft. 4 and wrestled bullies to the ground, he liked to read at night near the glow of the fireplace; he also freed the slaves and got shot. He was large, mythic, he never let me go.

But Sir Galahad, thru what induction I know not, grasped me more than any other. I think we don't choose our heroes. They choose us. Tintagel was so-so and I dislike the Middle Ages—evil theologians, torture chambers, serfs, T.S. Eliot, wrinkled folks in dunce caps hoeing dirt as dull as woodcuts. My instincts were pure Titian, Renaissance.

Yet Galahad sticks in my soul. "My strength is the strength of ten because my heart is pure." My first bookplates, which I printed in my father's shop, were after Watt's painting, a full profile, with Galahad's horse, far lovelier than Autry's. Years later I bought a copy for my sons. It's composed of butterscotch and violins, and Galahad's sword is bigger than any other sword in the world. To the constant shock of my cynicism and good taste, I cherish it.

And I hope he's hooked my sons. I hope they will be gentle men and kind to those in need; that they will know how to fight the monsters of injustice, deceit and despair; that they will be chevaliers, not grocers (though I have nothing against grocers); that they'll go after the Grail; that amidst all merriment I pray is theirs, they will be ultimately serious about ultimately serious things. And yes, be pure in heart, though this must finally mean more thorough understanding of their own participation in what Traherne called the dirty devices of this world.

But they will have their own heroes who'll visit them from the vasty deep and halls, as mine do with me. Hutson, Greenberg, Harmon, Autry, Flynn, Samson, the French horn players, Lincoln, Galahad—from Green Bay across Michigan to Israel, from the coast of Cornwall to Little Pigeon Creek between the Wabash and Ohio, the Christ is universal with faces enough and more.

RELUCTANT
CONFESSIONAL

Several confessionals I'd rather not make:

Pat Nixon is a lovely, lovely woman and did us proud in China. So did her what's-his-name.

The comparison between My-lai and Ulster drawn by my favorite Senator (Kennedy) is ridiculous.

I don't care how you cut it, a fetus is more than a piece of garbage. Liberals are too happy and virtuous about abortion. We can't take ambiguity. I fight/fought hard for abortion rights. Its use though—not as a backstop to contraception—but as a primary means of birth control is an offense against life. And cruel to couples who beg to adopt but can't because the liberated curette is too busy snuffing elfin miracles.

We need a new hymnal to replace the new hymnal. The Blue Book, bulging with Ken Patton's grandiose try harder utopian mysticism, wears woefully. Phrases like "Man is the earth upright and proud" sound more desperate and declamatory every year.

And my beloved Whitman can be wronger than Kennedy, like Number 429 announcing "sweet-blooded youth" and "splendid savage old men." Quintessence of putrescence, friends, pure puke. Spender's "I think continually" is a triumph, and some new hymns and tunes like 276,111.

But any hymnal with the guts to expunge The Battle Hymn Of The Republic and perpetuate Abide With Me ought to be shot at dawn right in the clef, without blindfold or cigarette.

U-Uers flying to Europe this summer instead of sailing on ships should have their passports revoked. And get shot at dawn, with jet planes and Abide With Me playing in the background.

Instead of firemen learning Portuguese, let the Portuguese learn English. We settled that one in 1588, praise the Lord.

I buried a young soldier recently, in a full military committal (rifle volleys, flags, marching, bugle, all). This ceremonial offering by 20 officers and uniformed men was lean, comprehending, purging, sustaining, utterly sensitive, perfectly moving. Must the Christian Church go to warriors to learn what great liturgy is about? (Try that one on for ambiguity.)

People who believe in God are infantile.

People who don't believe in God are narcissists.

IF I WERE THE POPE

In the refulgence of this high autumn I fancy myself the Pope. I interdict the passage of this splendid October and make a decretal against the further fall of leaves. In quietness and confidence I expel the snow and pronounce malediction on approaching winter's obliquity.

As I warm to my new tasks other papal projects come to mind, oblations I would do for the Church Universal. I must certainly interdict the planet in general for surliness and stupidity and announce opprobrium on almost everything, but let me be particular: excommunication for those who throw rocks at the President of the United States and banishment for those who think rock throwing is the source of the national malaise.

Censure on Russians who can't take their own writers, millionaires who don't like their taxes, and Spaniards and Greeks who support their governments. A small plague on the Pentagon for conduct unbefitting an army; the Post Office for its special issue on Stone Mountain; the Department of Justice for knowingly harboring and giving aid and comfort to J. Edgar Hoover. I sign philippics against the vice president and spank Angela Davis in a private audience.

Not everything I do is negative, although a little vilifying, extraditing, anathematizing, obloquy and execration from the Pontiff never hurt anybody. I erect a new ceiling and commission Picasso; hold country dances in the Basilica and engineer assignations between Italian Communists and touring Dutch nuns; export chianti to Castro and revolution to Capetown; sack priests who sacramentalize the privilege of wealth and raise up leftists in South America who care for Christ. I spend time in Cairo and Jerusalem.

I summon the Beatles for a second crusade against the Blue Meanies, elevate Muhammad Ali to the editorship of L'Osservatore Romano, demand an end to state aid to parochial schools; canonize Margaret Sanger, Sherry Fishbine, Harry Truman and W.C. Fields; consign Lester Maddox to the icy regions of the Inferno; make an ecumenical call on Bob West and kiss his shiny Jack Armstrong secret-code message-container ring. Beyond this I present the Heissmann trophy to the third-string right tackle of the Utah College of Mines and Optometry; serve champagne, London broil, and pretty women to all prisoners everywhere held in jail for lack fo bail, and in other ways demonstrate the gospel claim that the meek shall inherit the earth.

In foreign policy I send my SSG (Secret Service Guard) to pull off an exhumatory heist of Henry VIII's bones, which I hold for ransom. The ensuing expenditure, emotional and economic, will start an Anglican revival and revitalize the empire in that land of my second love. I take Egg Foo Yong on Easter and rice and saki for mass, toss the tiara in the Tiber, exile aides who believe God is a Neapolitan, objurate oil slicks, commend pornography to cure the lewd minds of curia censors, and compel all priests to marry at least on a trial basis.

I close my day in quiet prayer and a stroll in my 107.8-acre garden realm. Before retiring I write a note to my friend Richard Nixon telling him that the next time he visits Rome in an aircraft carrier and starts flattering me about how much spiritual power I possess, I'll humbly sink his goddam ship.

Finally I begin beatification rites for John XXIII, and proscribe and drum out Paul VI on grounds of timidity and lack of faith.

IN MEMORIAM: GEO. LEWIS

I miss your sound, George
I miss you, eyes deep and sad,
chocolate veins, talc
      and shining face,
collar too big and white,
      a frame,
holding all thinness, you.
So gentle
your fingers,
moons piping the
stopped and blue-ing sky.
So full of wood, your clarinet,
      and pumice, herbs.
I hope it's not encased
in a dixieland hall of fame,
that this woodwind plays still,
gentle as your voice and art,
for funerals, vespers,
whores, New Orleans nights.
Not for the´rich daughters
      of the north.

WHOLLY OTHER

Church towers and sky-scrapers
Shine to light webs of men and credit
Strutting invisibly between the Capitol
    and oil derricks.
The city builds high, pulls hard
        on bells
        beams
        soil
        ledgers
Louder and higher and harder with the work
    of its hands
Because it is a still night in Oklahoma
And noise-grated bugs coast on prairie dark.

ORIGINAL SIN

Last night TV—Haiti, Papa Doc, wicked black man like Hitler.
Sons of Amos refused me to bury a parishoner in their soil.
Plus Arabs assassinate.
Scots (that's me) kill with the best of them
(I learned this with a Rogerian, not Freud)
Any group with a toehold grows obnoxious.
England who saved title deeds of right spat fire on Dresden,
Jesus Christ forgive us all, or God, somebody.
If Swedes are nice it's they hadn't the option.
And lovely Mao, poet, last of the great executioners.
Even great Monticello's edge stank with bondage.
Oh Thomas, oh my Lincoln,
Wicked Wilson who died for dreams,
Roosevelt, hurting the sweet strong lady,
And Angela, Angela, don't trust the manifesto,
Blessed people the disease is deep.
God forgive us all,
Spare thou those who are penitent.
The rest we'll kill ourselves.

GIMMIE THAT OLD...

The Unseen Tide
The preacher said
Moves on the side of Right.
The preacher's son
Who went to fight
Hardly will deny it,
Being dead.

TIME

the Life
that maketh
all things new
maketh
all things
quaint

OCTOBER

Octobers I played football, most
Games on Michigan nights
And bonfire smells. An ordinance now I suppose.
The Kalamazoo river stank through my town
But chill autumn cleansed it to fog and mist
Behind the lights that lighted our field.
My father watched on Father's Night,
Number 47 pinned to pungent wool.
In October I grieve my father's death
and memories of that field are green.

October is my favorite month. Its splendor
Tears but the pain, like lust, is sweet.
God made October to keep us quite alive.
He made October to push the limits back,
A wedge to open the core of hearts.
''How much can man take without falling apart?
Let's see—Give him October.''

And now the incomparable summons,
Pumpkins, gourds, footballs,
V-wedge of ducks (I shot only one blue wing teel)
Joys of apples, costumes, Hallowe'en,
And in the bursting clarity of high autumn
We lived and now pray for all souls and our own.

This confusion in one's arms,
This grace of harvest, and great resignings,
O October shatters us alive. Dear God
we wonder to laugh, lament, shout praise or cry.

BIRTHDAY

Thirty years to pound the crooked arches
of the heart; (vast labors)
I walk at thirty with the immense light gift,
wrested from the pumped days,
the blood years, the dark wood's edge.

Declare now the moratorium on the burning bush—
sleep my evil, rest the raging saint's brain,
the sleepless eye,
the wounded ribs of love.

Do not despise the broken years,
thrown across populous curving cinders,
measured and choked in the world's chalk,
and lunged in the heart of the Milky Way.

Only rest now deeply awhile.
Good-bye to God's hammered doors,
the sudden terror, the desperate choice,
Good-bye to my own 'great courage,
no longer needed, nor Beatrice, nor perfection.

I walk at thirty
in the crooked arches of the heart
tolerant for chaos and my death
home in the hours
with the immense light gift.

RETROSPECT

The suns open my inland birth,
Lighten shamed days, the valley cage,
And all the framed rectitudes of
The struggle and catapult years.

Swum in salt, fathomed clean,
I walk later years in my town,
Flushed of fools and elder spleen,
Forgiven all prisoner guilt.

My footsteps home are sounds in praise.
No one locked up that summer night
Of rough games, sky, our great boy shouts
When Borealis crashed like noon.

HOP, O LAZY SPENSERIAN SONNET, HOP!

One of many moguls
Jumping at clocks
Scratching his skull
Searching for socks
Phoning in stocks
Shouting from toilet
Waving his cock
Reading his gazette
Hedging his bet
Mixing juice
Rushing for jet
Cutting loose
　　　What's the meaning
　　　Of this careening?

THRENODIC TRIOLET
FOR US CLERGY

Obituary headlines gall
    Announcing pastors passing.
Priests and preachers all in thrall,
Obituary headlines gall.
I'll turn down any call
    Reading this cosmic thrashing.
Obituary headlines gall
Announcing pastors passing.

LIFEGUARD

Burnt gilt belly, undulant avatar,
Lured in spindrift to the stunning beach,
Swing high sienna thighs dancing afar.

On this wind-strummed bay by a singing spar
I flame in sulphur of the sanding reach,
Burnt gilt belly, undulant avatar.

Your high August body a seminar
Of caramel tortures, limbs sweet to teach,
Swing high, sienna thighs, dancing afar.

A grocery of lust thy sunned bazaar,
Fretted with saffron and honeyed peach,
Burnt gilt, belly undulant, avatar.

To your dear descending in gulls and star
Tongues lick up, forever to beseech,
Swing, high sienna thighs dancing afar.

But love's seasons end and a foreign car
Carries you inland from flood tides of speech,
Burnt gilt belly, undulant avatar,
Swing high, sienna thighs, dancing afar.

LITURGY

competent
cogent
scorning ritual,
the occult,
all truth by reason

one heavy night
she
whipped
him

magic
after
that

Uncollected
Pieces

DON'T GIVE AN INCH!

This is a protest and lamentation over the metrication of the world, the final triumph of the 1791 adoption by the French Assembly of the report of the Paris Academy of Sciences, the Age of Reason's attempt to objectify our world. The metric system is obligatory or pushing ahead everywhere, including the USA since the Metric Conversion Act was passed by Congress in 1975, a date that should live in infamy. You give a Frenchman a millimeter and he'll take a kilometer.

We should have hit them harder at Waterloo—a gram of prevention then would have been worth a kilogram of cure today.

We'll soon be metricized in our supermarkets, on our highways, and in our bedrooms. No more 9 by 12 rugs, 9.4-men or 6'8" centers. No more loving a bushel and a peck, no more 16 inch guns, no more walking 1.6093 for a Camel. And probably no more poems—"I have promises to keep and kilometers to go before I sleep?" That frosts the blood.

The metric system—the colorless Esperanto of weights and measures—has won the day. I don't know why. We have conversion tables, translations, and in the world of technical measurements, science already has its accurate, efficient, if dessicated, language. Why can't they keep it in their laboratories instead of shoving it into our kitchens?

I suspect that metrication has come to make it easier for an auto mechanic to repair a Volkswagen in Utah with a six millimeter wrench. Or so that rifles and missiles can be interchanged among combatants without backfire or embarrassment or inconvenience to the weapons industry and the State Department.

In my book a meter is an overextended yard, exactly three and 37-100ths of an inch wrong. I do not believe in celsius or milliliters or hectometers. I believe in inches, cups, furlongs, ounces, carets, gills, firkins, acres, ricks and rods, drams and cords.

I affirm dozens, quires, long tons, pennyweights, hogsheads and jeroboams. I believe in a non-metric world, full fathoms five, various, beautiful, new. I resist the objectification and thingification of our space and heft and history.

Metric measure has its sub-human and icy origins in 1,650,763.73 wave lengths of an orangish light given off by an obscure gas, Krypton 86. A foot at least comes from a human foot, an inch from three barleycorns of food.

Our yard is the muscled arm of Henry the First, from the point of his nose to the end of his Thumb. Krypton 86 is a fall from human grace. I'll take Henry over Krypton any day. So raise a toast with a split, a bottle, a magnum or a rehoboam, or hell, why not a nebuchadnezzar (four gallons, one pint and thirteen ounces): Don't give an inch—the Age of Reason is miles wrong!

FESTIVAL IN THE CHURCH FOR JLA

In largeness of heart and sweep of mind
none of us knows his equal.
Even with our preening egos
we would all place him on the highest level
except
he'd whip us for idolatry and wasting time.

So we send our more modest praise
to our beloved Churchman and brother
and leave for later scholars to marvel
on this typological wonder.

For between Marburg, Chicago, Oxford, et al.,
he's belonged to us, ministering on back stoops
and by letter and in Church kitchens to 4 a.m.
a pouring-out pleroma,
making us shy and great as kings and queens.
(In this Leveller's polity all are enthroned.)

We thank him for staying with us, our pitiable sect;
for loving the Church and wringing its neck;
for helping us read Plato and Amos and Bach,
and the suffering in other rooms;
for helping human groups to find their powers;
for shaking the foundations of this rotten state;
and remembering our children's names.

Accept, please, this festival gift, O Lord,
for this man's frame and flesh,
for his forehead, stubby hands, pug nose, sweet face,
for his kindness, action, drama,
and window to your grace.

BE MY VALENTINE

A billet-doux from St. Valentine to all UUs—144,832 of you in one of the most miniscule denominations you'll ever find. For survival, comeback, the new day, in your 1,000 unique societies, happy Valentine's Day!

But we'd not confine our Valentine wishes to the chic provincialism of the present tense and now. We send sweet dispatches across the years: to the valley of the Maros (in 1579) and the cold dungeon at Deva where our Francis died; to the ember place in Geneva where no hearts went out to Michael; to the shattered lab of Priestley and the Selma street where Jim went down. Rainbowy valentines to the grave and gone, arching gravestones at Sleepy Hollow for voluble Ralph, in Florence over Theodore, at Mt. Auburn for Messrs. Channing, Murray and Ballou.

Bigger valentines yet to the likes of Philip Wickstead and Henry Bellows and a closet full of women, the greater and neglected saints who, like most saints, seldom get the credit they deserve. Huge valentines to you who serve in Church and Fellowship without notice or applause, who open the doors and turn off the lights; who hang in decade after decade; who do the essential and undramatic work, e.g., achieving the goal of the annual fund.

Valentines to UUs out of step with orthodoxies, including a house brand of our own that's about as subtle as the Spanish Inquisition. Heartfelt notes to those who have tasted guilt and found it real, who trusted to goodness and got beat up really good, who must yet learn that not reason and not Esalen can free us from the ambiguities in human encounter. A valentine of forgiveness to a people who aren't fond of the world.

Valentines to the 167 widows listed in the Directory and to the 2,548 members we lost last year. (A smudgy, torn valentine to the evangelicals—we'll build churches in their wake.) Penny valentines to every one of our 41,321 children in Church School—stay with us, young hearts, we need you around.

Hearty hearts to the 120 societies benefitting from UUA loans, with an italic nudge on the back that "Reciprocal love is yummiest." Loving lines to the 61 women studying for our ministry who shine now in no reflected moon, but stand in their own sun, sweating like Sappho.

Love letter to you, little brother-sisterhood, to keep fresh and human the human way, institutions of caring and justice and long mythic memory against the giant and February cold. May Wordsworth's words be inscribed for you and the Liberal Church: "Its exterior semblance did belie its soul's immensity."

Be my valentine.